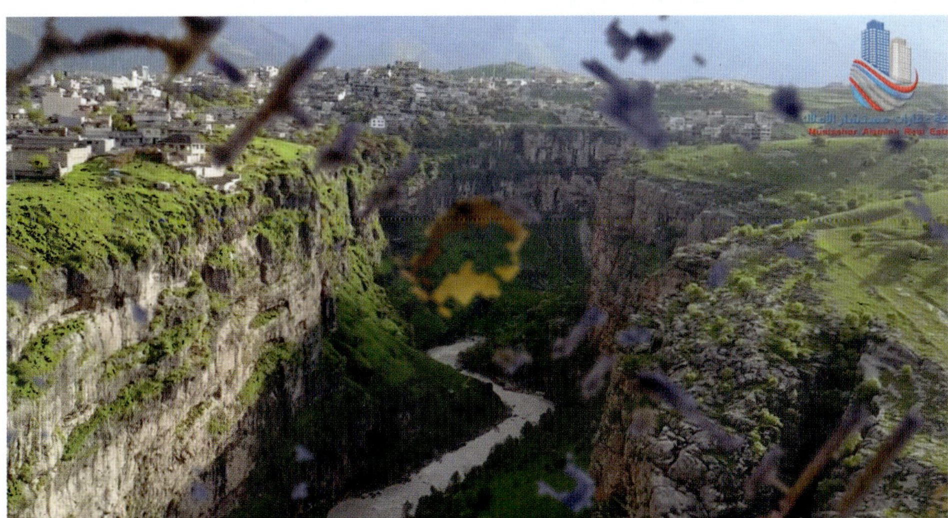

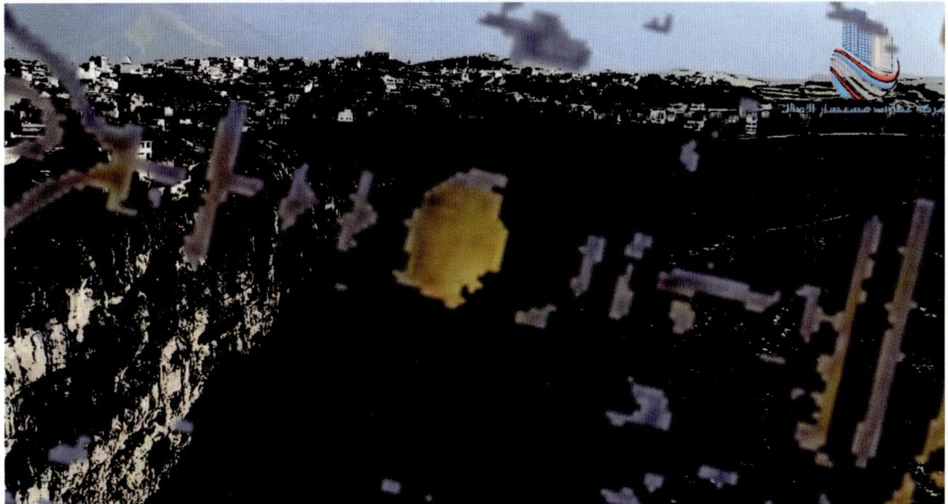

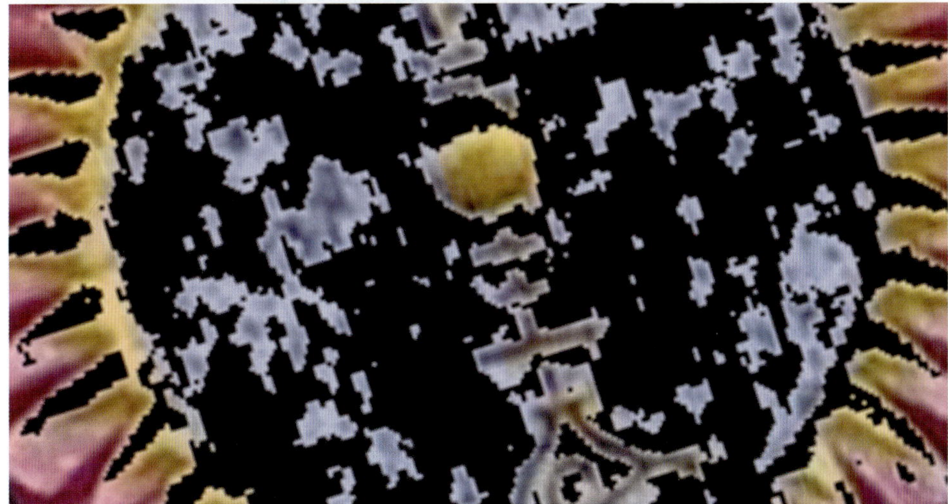

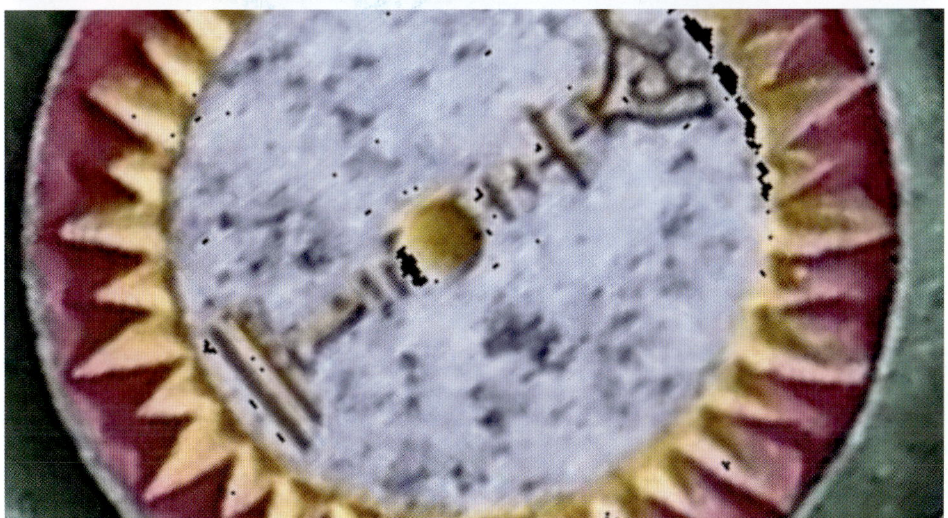

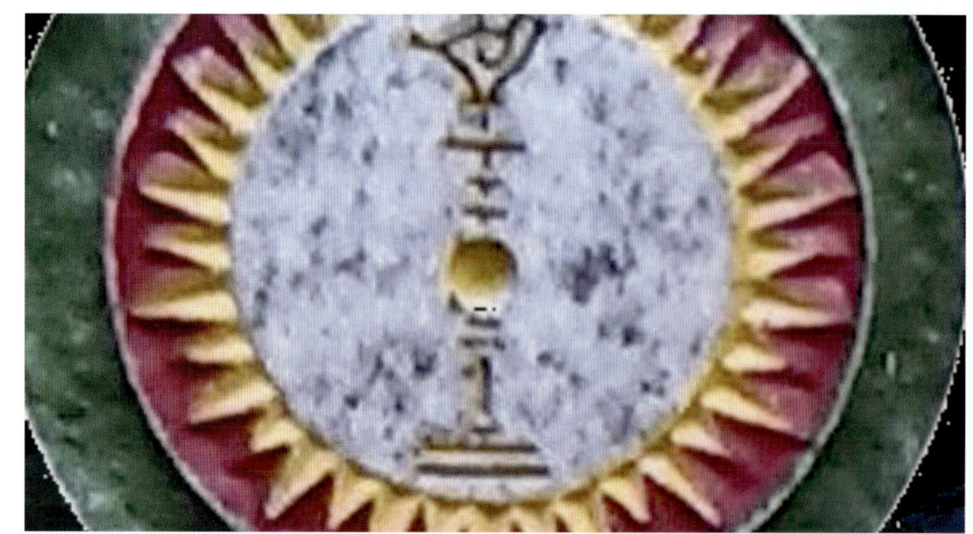

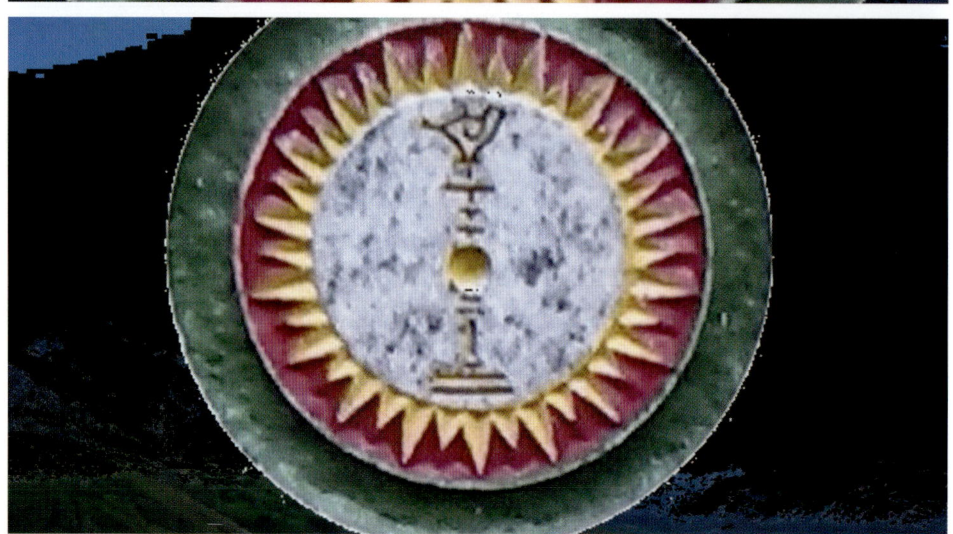

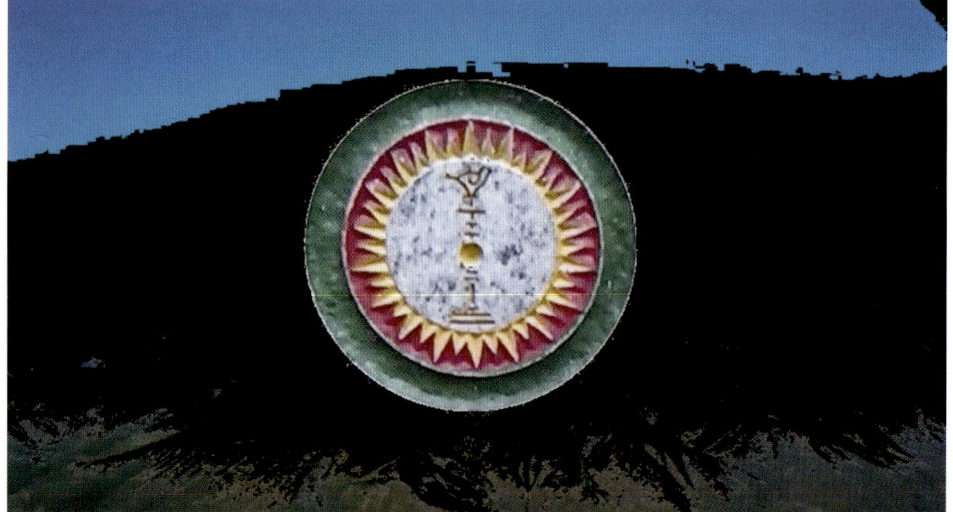

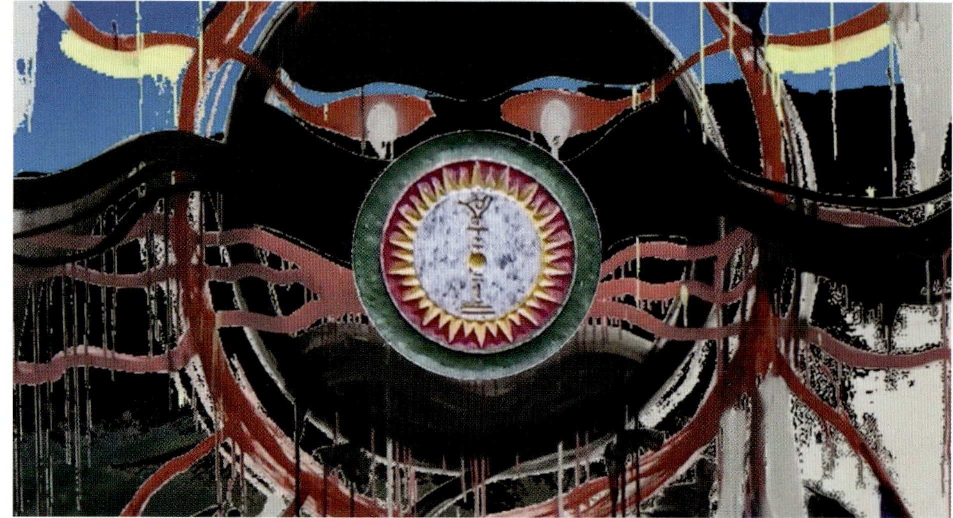

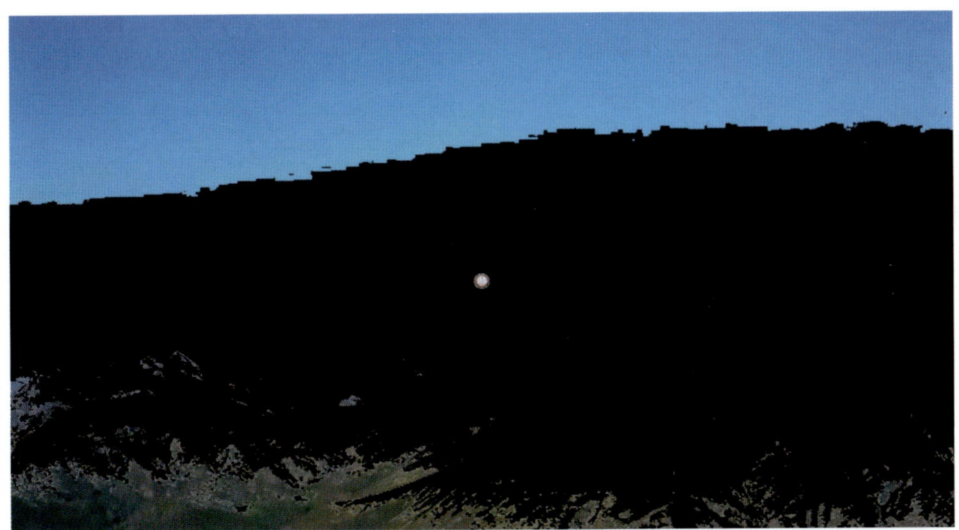

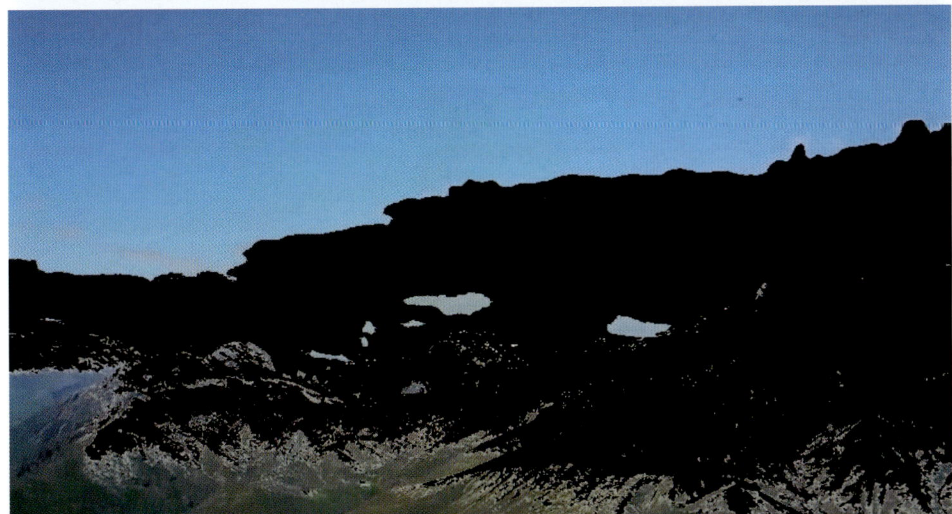

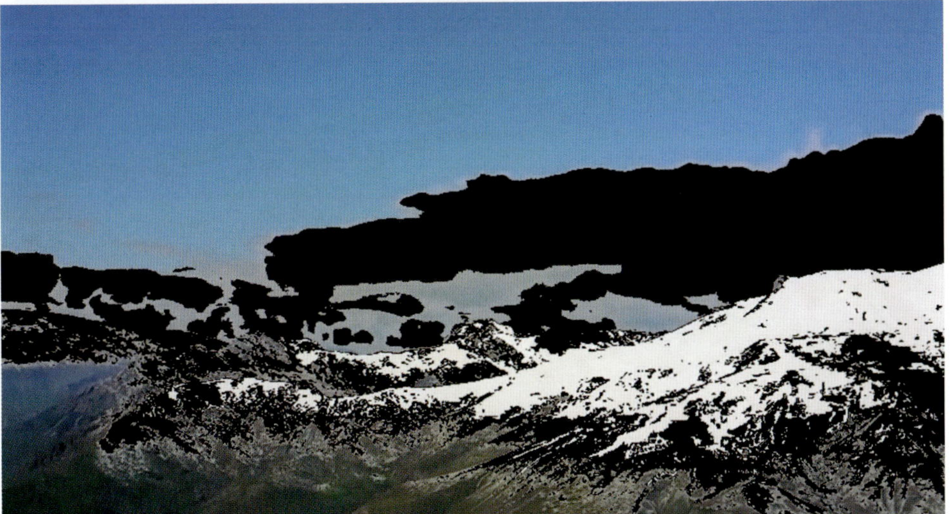

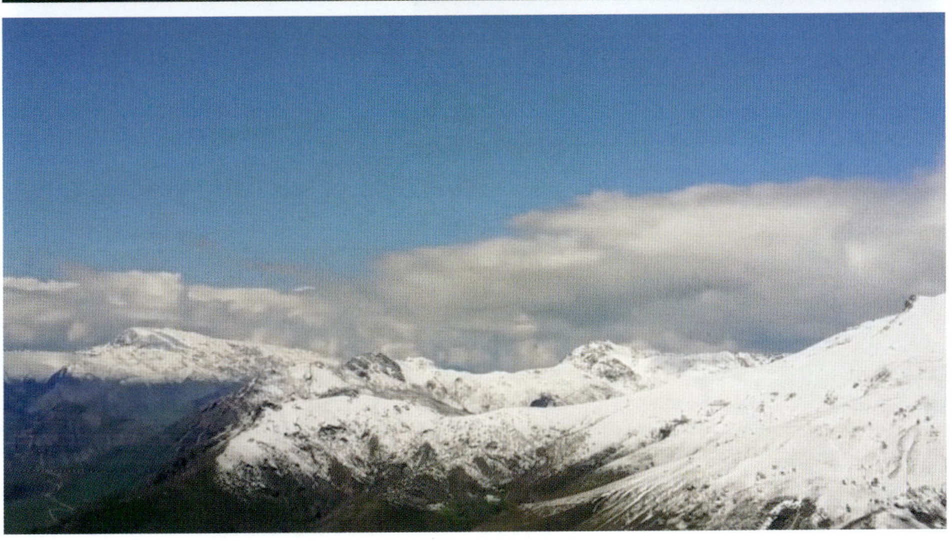

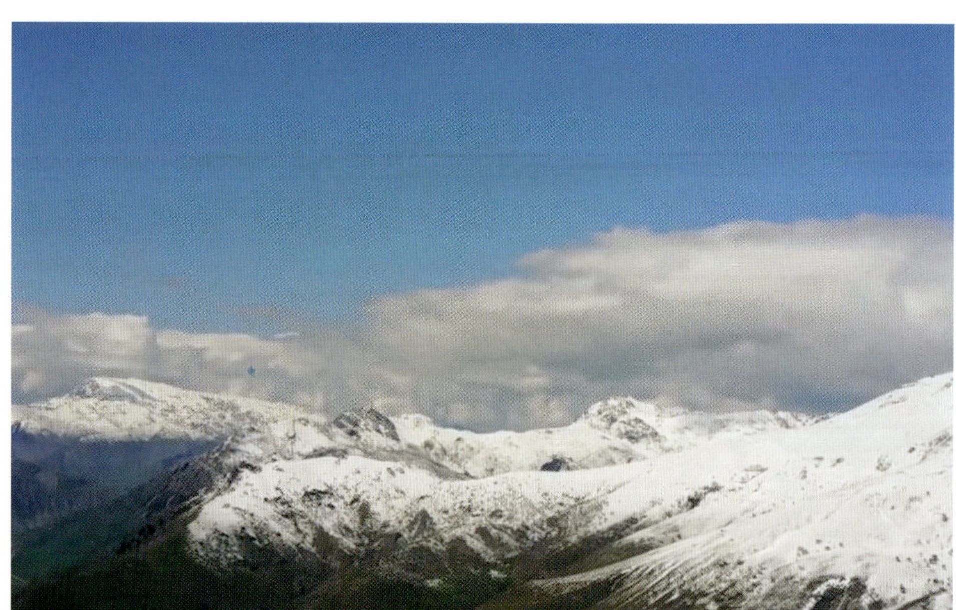
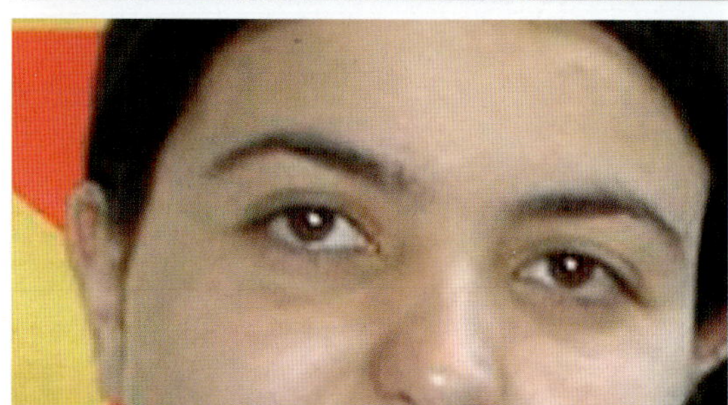
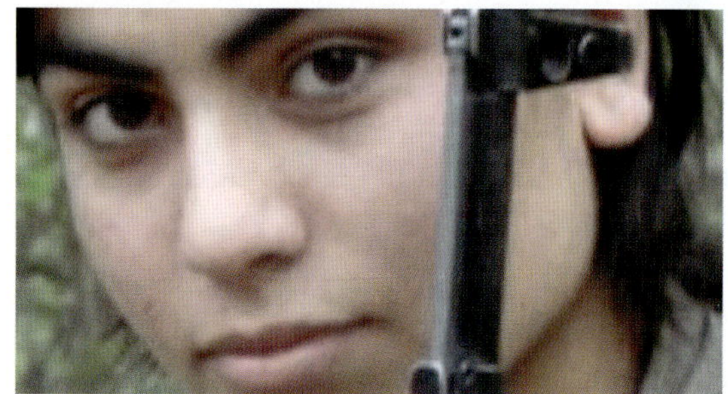
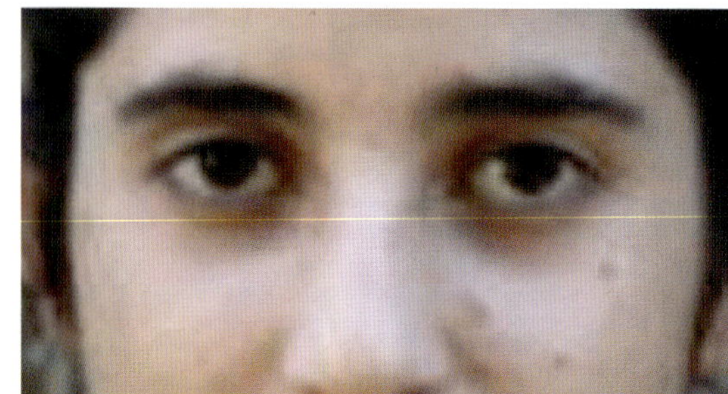
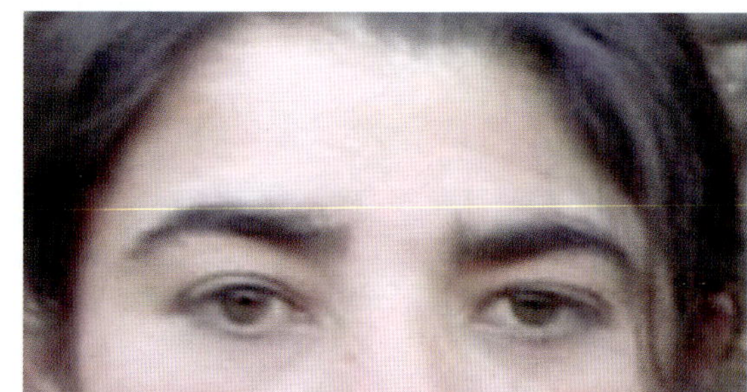
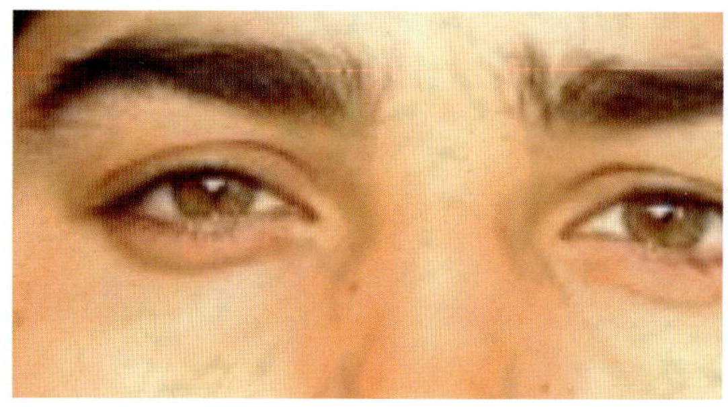
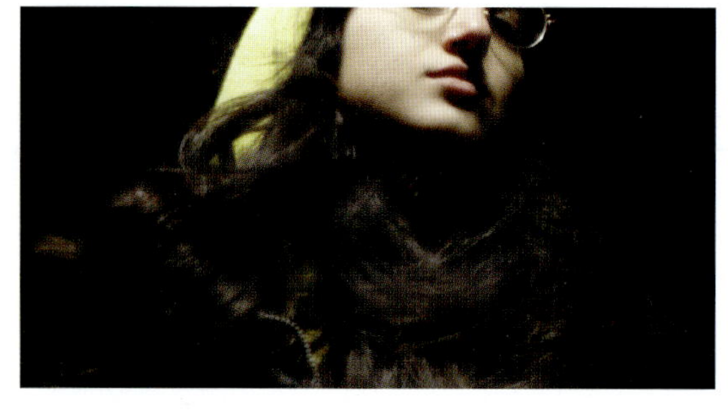
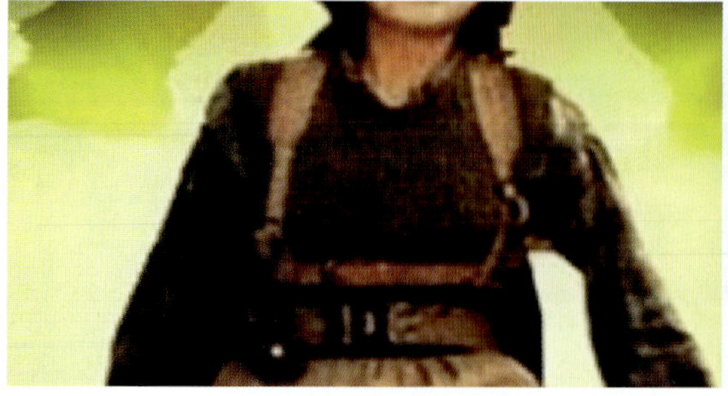

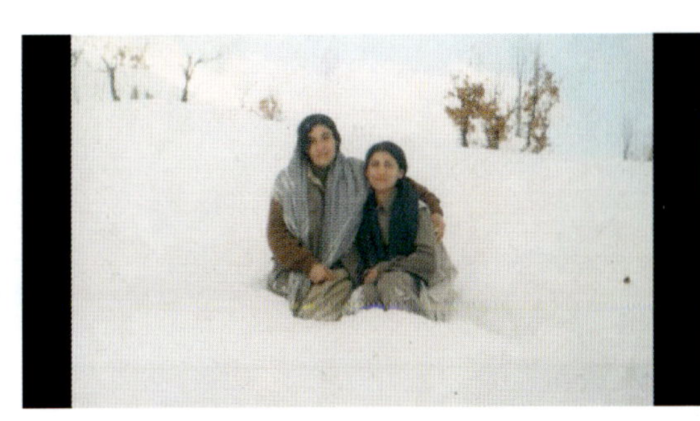
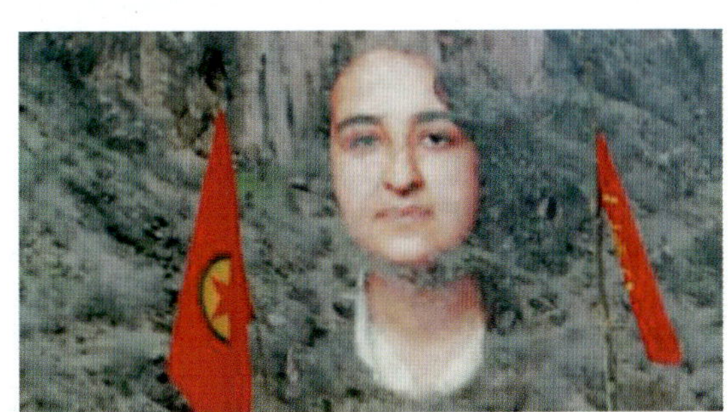
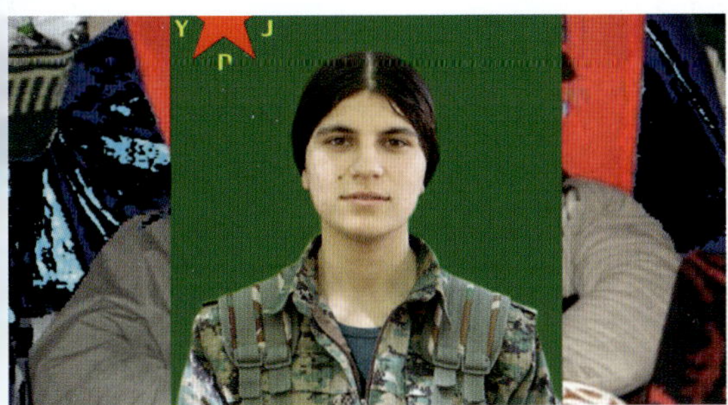
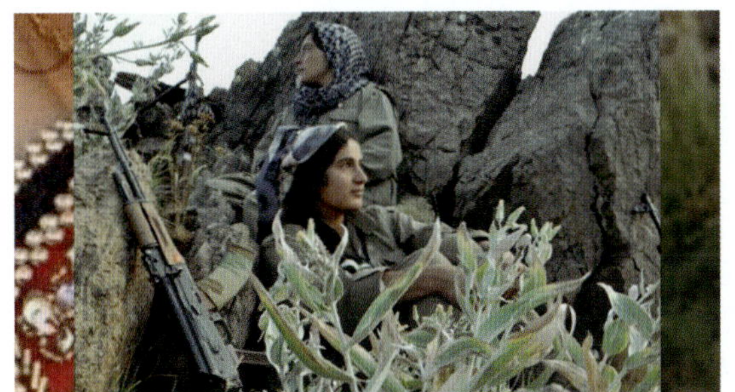
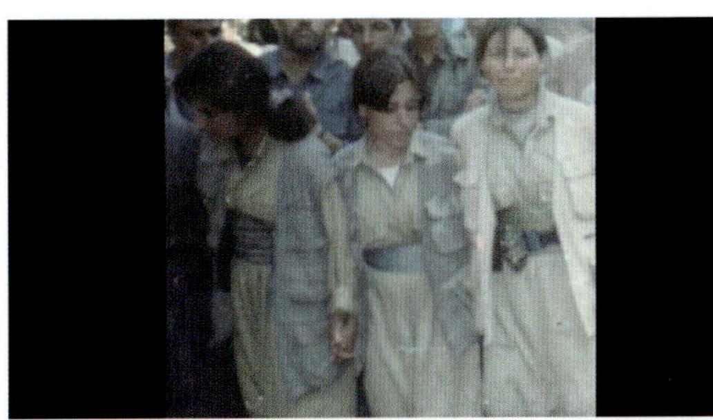
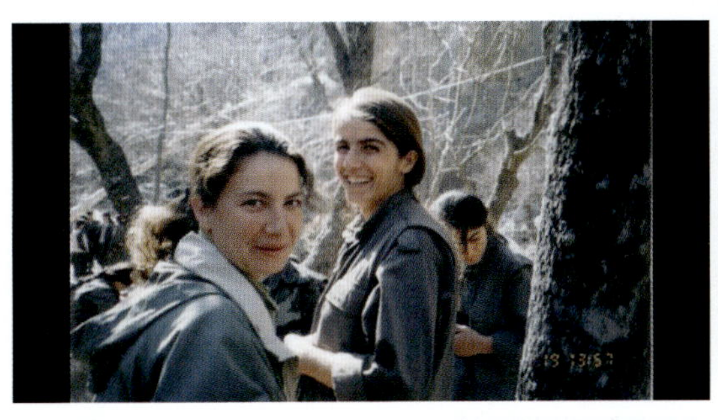
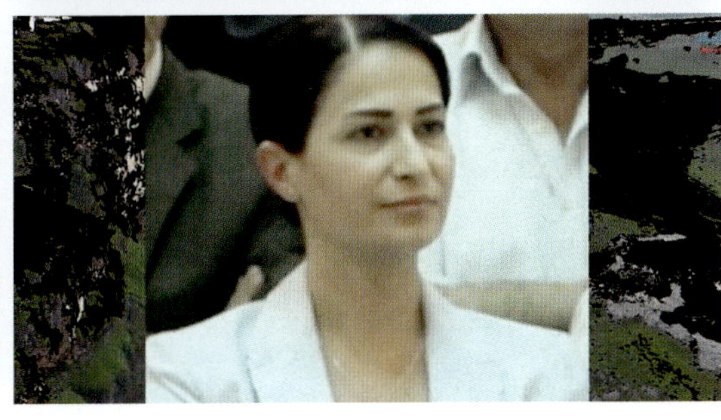
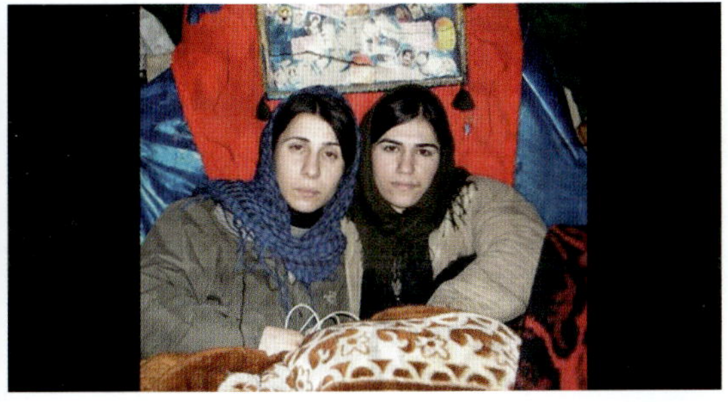

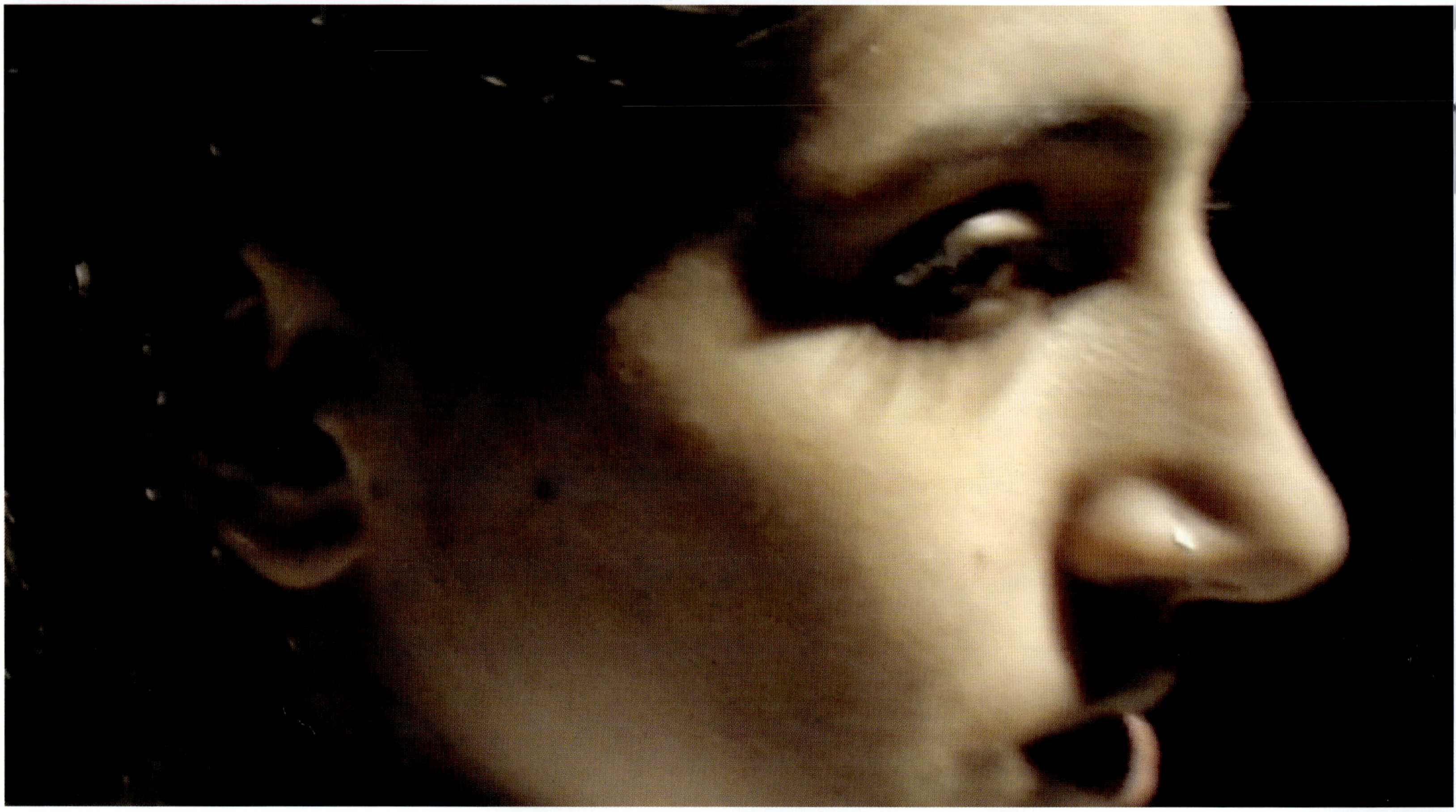

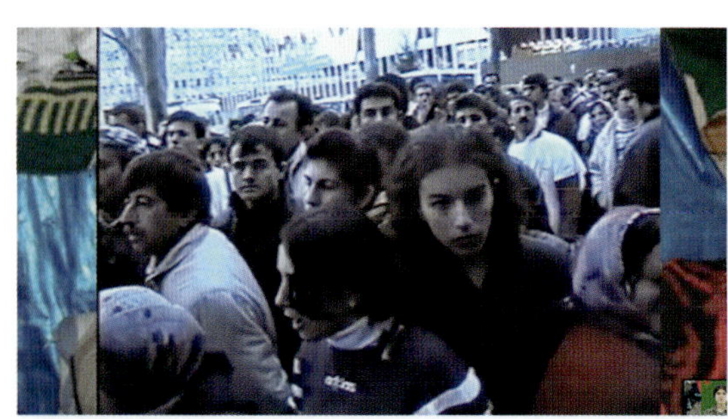
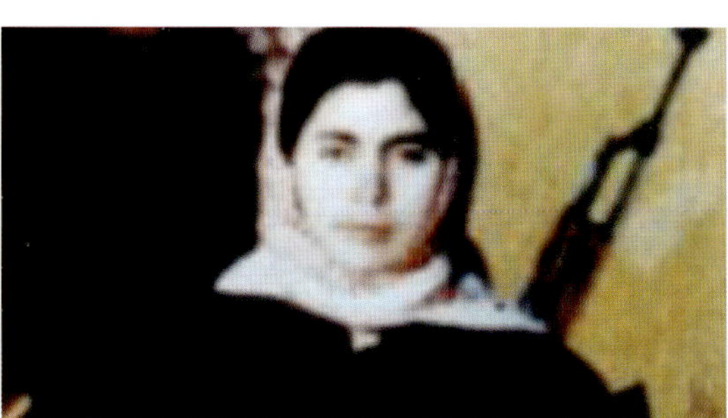
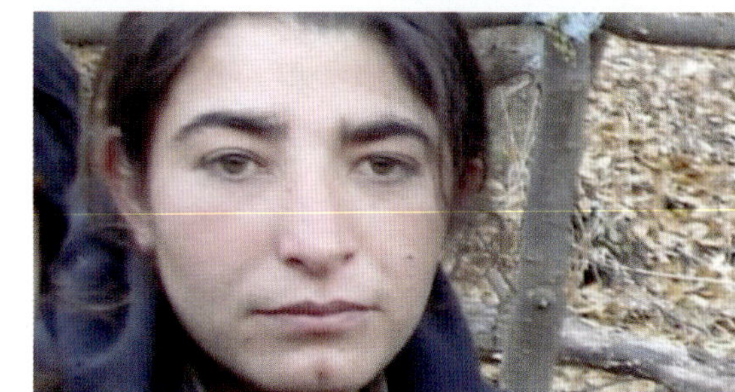
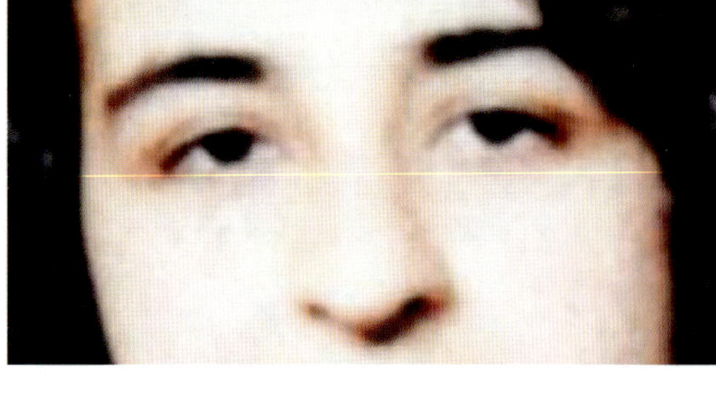
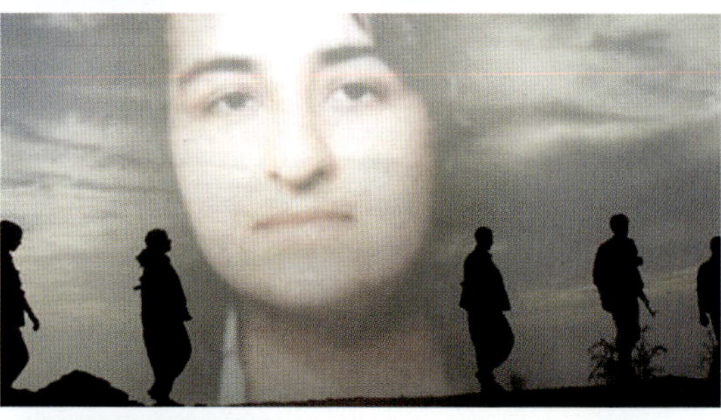
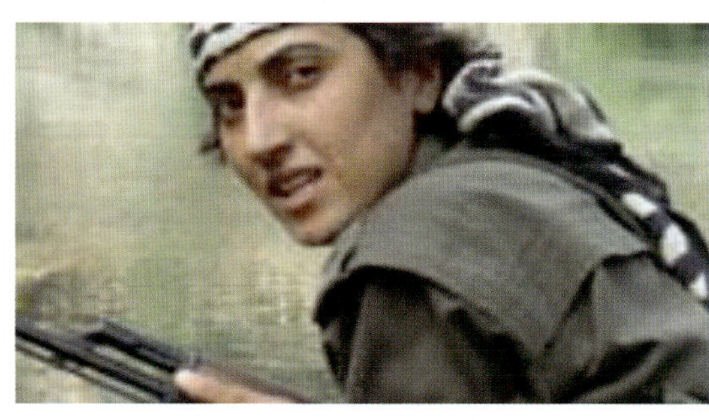
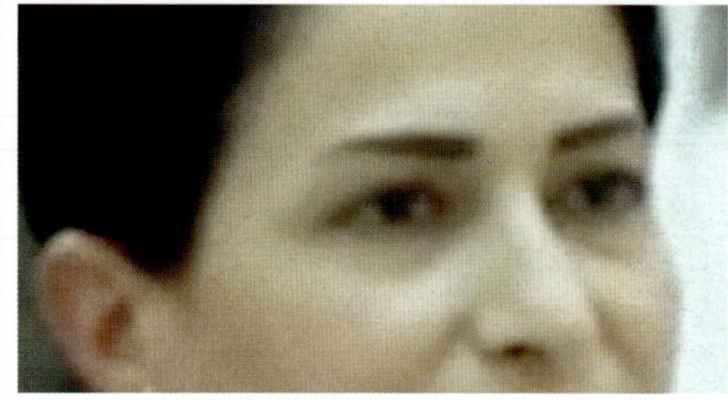

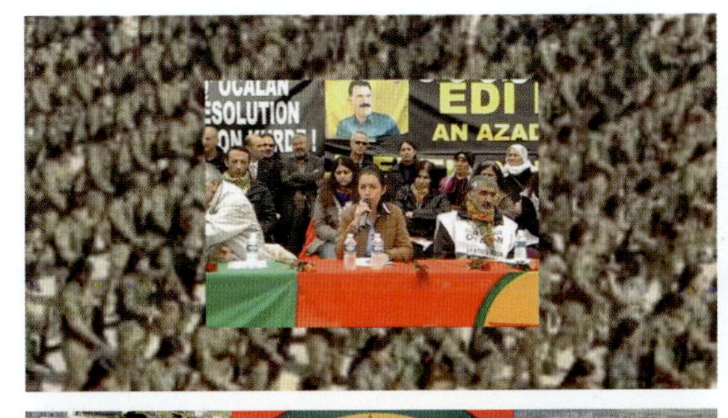
OCALAN
ESOLUTION
ON KURD
EDI
AN AZAD

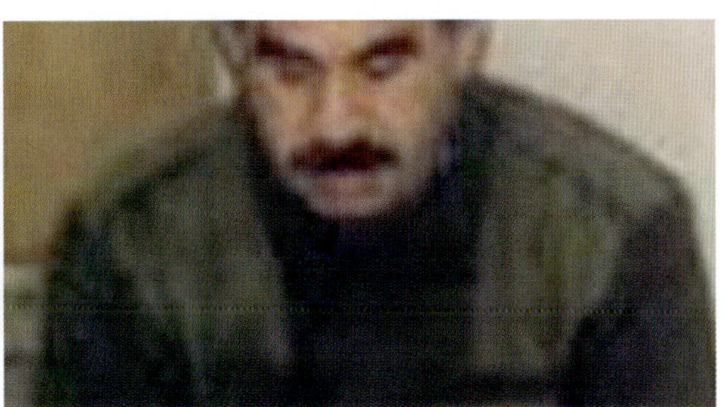

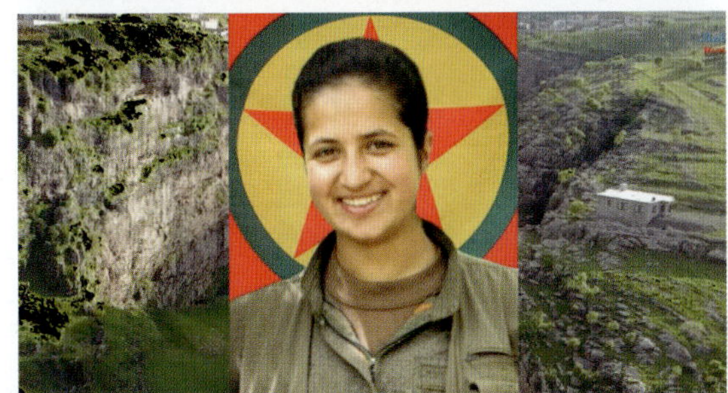

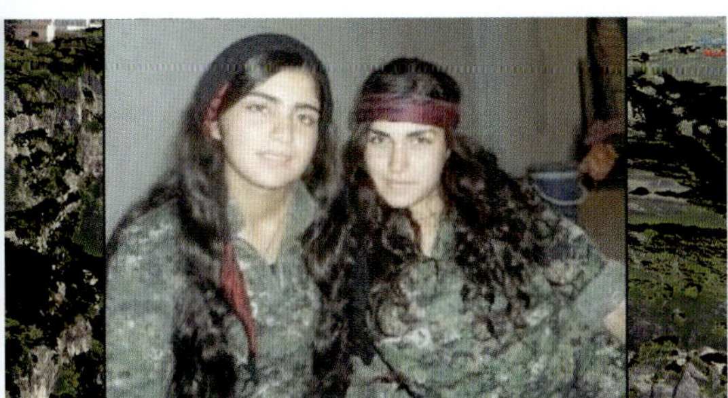

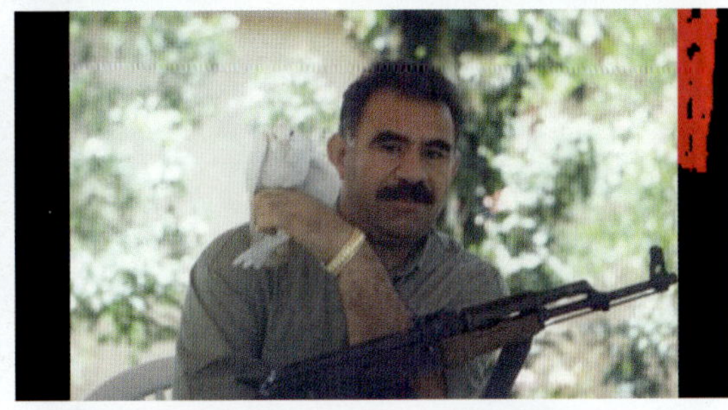

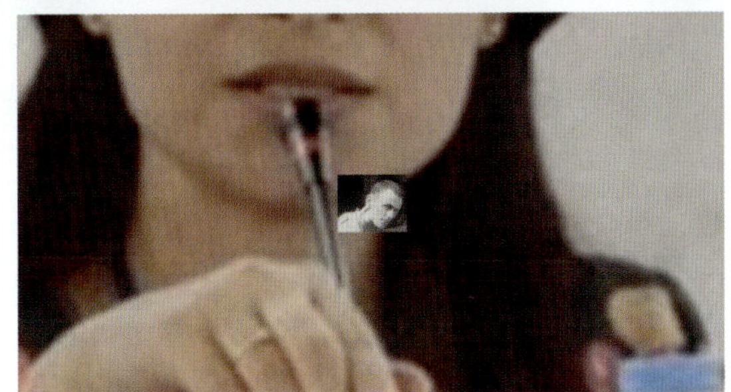

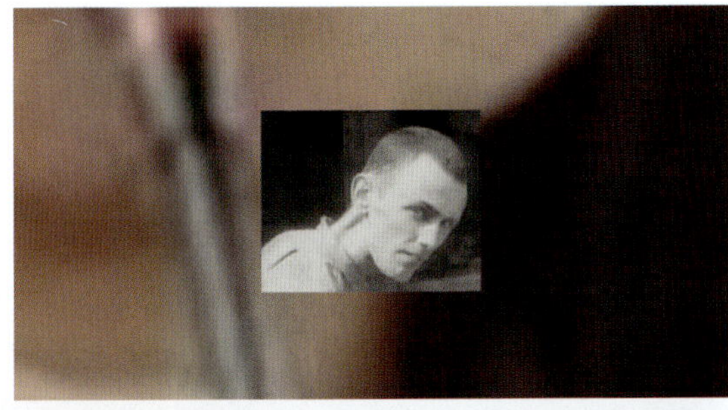

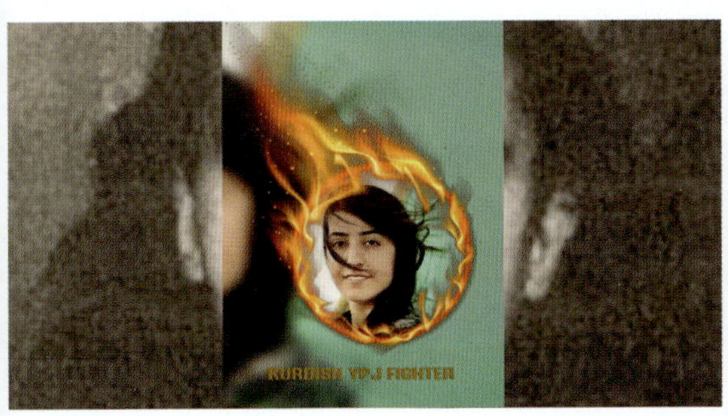
KURDISH YPJ FIGHTER

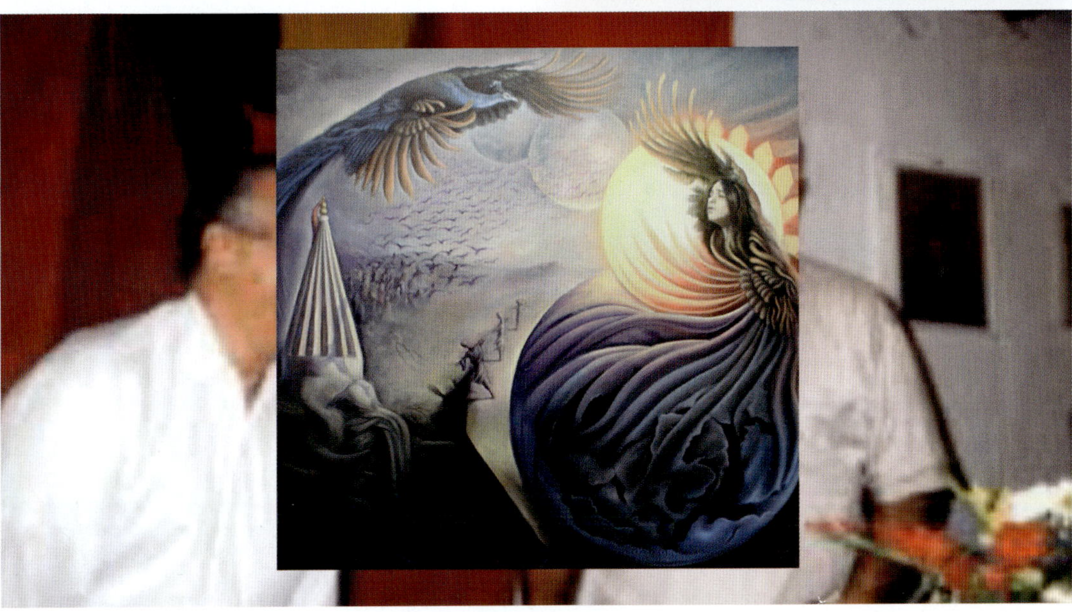

Mousse Publishing   Kunsthaus Hamburg

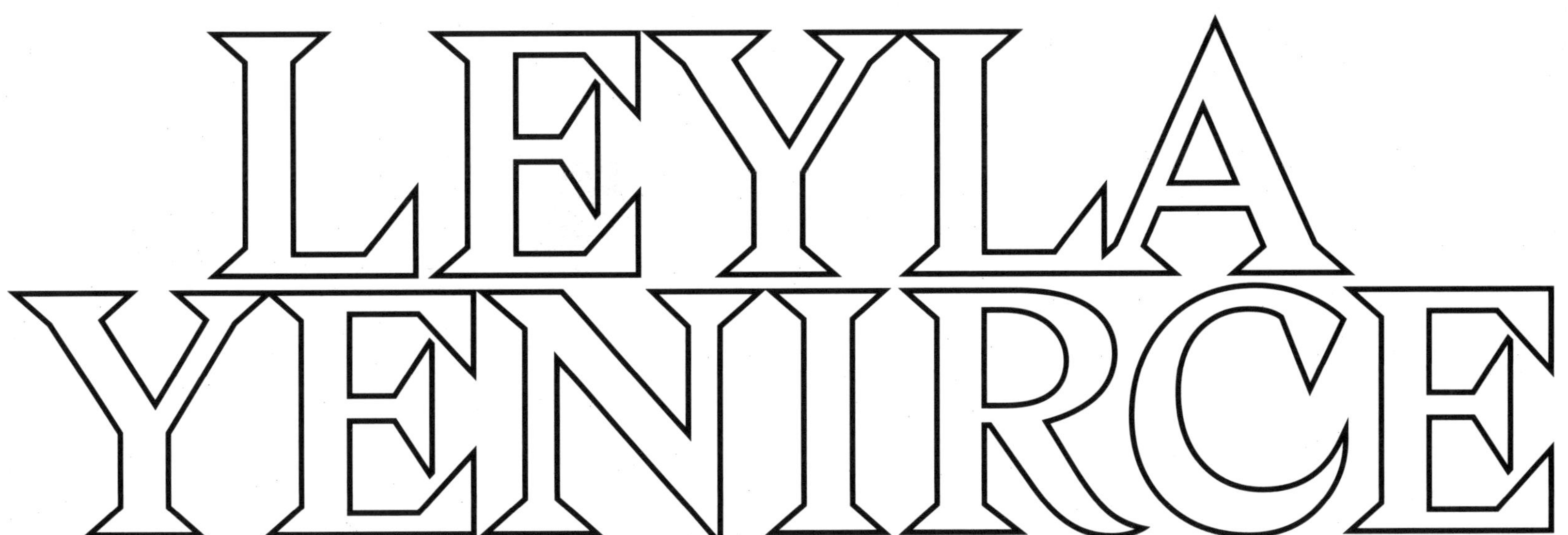

This publication was supported as Catalogue No. 153 by the Alfried Krupp von Bohlen und Halbach-Stiftung under its support prize "Catalogues for Young Artists."

Diese Publikation wurde als 153. Katalog von der Alfried Krupp von Bohlen und Halbach-Stiftung im Rahmen des Förderpreises „Kataloge für junge Künstler*innen" gefördert.

TABLE OF CONTENTS / INHALTSVERZEICHNIS

TEXTS / TEXTE

IF ONLY I KNEW HOW
TO DISAPPEAR

Mazlum Nergiz

*If only I knew how to disappear, there would be a perfect union of love between
God and the earth I tread, the sea I hear.*   Simone Weil

The Buenos Aires Japanese Gardens are located about 40 minutes south-
east of the murky Río de la Plata. A Sunday in December. The vast grey
sky is covered by tattered clouds, drifting low over the city. The vague
wind also drives Mará and me away from the Río, which is as wide as if
it had no shore.
Oceans are aimless. Rivers are not.
Mará is an old school friend of Juan, my husband. They both grew up in
Berazategui, a small town in the huge periphery of Buenos Aires. Walking
along Avenida Casares, Mará tells me that Berazategui is the capital of
glass. Capital of glass? "Yes, the Argentine glass industry settled there early
on. No idea why. There's also been a municipal glass school there since
1998. It's the only one in all of Latin America." Mará is wearing a lemon-
coloured tank top and very short shorts. Long, black hair that falls smoothly.
Her flip-flops scrape the pavement. Mará and I met two hours ago. Since
then she hasn't taken off her sunglasses. That's why it's hard for me to
describe her eyes. What I do see are dark brown freckles. I also see some
slightly lighter spots on her chapped, full lips.
Ever since my mother tried to hang herself in our garden—and
I had to tie her off together with my father—I have avoided gardens of any kind. Unfortunately, on our walk to the Japanese
Gardens, I missed the opportunity to postpone the visit. As we
stand in front of the entrance to the Jardín Japonés de la Ciudad
de Buenos Aires, I suggest that we'd better go to Berazategui.
Mará laughs. "What are we going to do in Berazategui?"
Juan and his sister went to see the cattle they bought two years ago, which
are looked after by a breeder. Whenever he is in Argentina, they go to visit
the cattle for a few days. I don't know what exactly they do there for so long.
I had seen pictures of the farm and decided not to go.
My mother taught me to play the cello when I was seven years
old. She wanted to teach me how to listen. "You have to feel how
the sound approaches, how it comes, passes, expands and pen-
etrates through you. Although I had great difficulty in reading
music, I thought I understood when she explained that while
the sound did not hide its face, it could not be seized either:
"It is all in front and behind, outside, inside, underneath and
above you, everywhere, like a ghost." My father accused her of
spoiling the instrument for me with these digressions, and why
wouldn't we just practise? I think she wanted to explain to me
that there are spaces I can't see, only hear.
Mará heads to the cash register and comes back with two blue paper
coupons that look like drink vouchers. "You can go to Berazategui with
Juan." She gives me my ticket and lines up in the short queue. The glare
of the sun now hitting us turns Mará and the others who are waiting
into overexposed shadows. I hold my ticket tightly between my thumb

and forefinger. The honking of the cars dissolves into one long sound. Mará comes back and takes me by the hand, like a small child forgotten by inattentive parents.

Night and Dreams by Franz Schubert was my mother's favourite piece. A song for one voice and piano. She got the version for piano and cello. She wanted us to play the piece together. I was expected to teach myself, within a month's time. Then she would accompany me on the piano. The piece was much too difficult for me. On the day we were supposed to make music together, my mother came home earlier than usual. She put the shopping on the table and called my father. She told him that the tumour in her breast was so big that it was already growing through the chest wall. The lesson was held anyway. My mother played the piano and I listened to her. Four months later she died.

Once my mother said, "When you play, you have to make a connection with yourself as an Other." What did she mean? Was she talking about ecstasy? Music as an attempt to transcend my body without leaving it?

In Mesopotamia the ecstatic state was described as maḫû, "being out of one's mind, mad; racing." In the Greek world there are three terms for it: enthusiasmós, having God in oneself, manía, madness, and later ékstasis, being beside oneself. In Ancient Rome, hardly any terms existed for ecstasy; even the given terminology is pejorative: furor. Official Christian teaching has nothing to offer either, apart from ecstatic women being cured in the New Testament and, in the Acts of the Saints, defined as possessed by demons. But we know, for example, the famed mystic Teresa from the Spanish Province of Ávila, of whom part of a rotting middle finger is on display in one of the convents. Teresa, whose heart was pierced by an angel appearing to her. When her body was exhumed in 1582, it was presumably found completely intact. It was removed, and then one thought to see a real wound in the heart, caused by the angel's spear. Today, her heart lies in a golden casket in the Convento de la Anunciación in Alba de Tormes.

What I forgot to ask her: Where is this Other of my Self when I happen not to be listening?

The Jardín Japonés is laid out around a lake. Shapeless, wildly contorting floss silk trees boasting pink petals line the path. Their barks are pierced with thorns. They take turns with elegant tepee trees, branches stretching wide, feathery leaves, bright yellow flowers. In the lake there lies a small island planted with medicinal herbs from Japan. Two short bridges lead to it. We pass a miniature replica of the Shurei-mon. Mará sits down on a stone pedestal opposite the copy of the famous entrance gate on Okinawa that leads one to Shuri Castle. Four pillars support the two superimposed roofs. Her right leg hurts, Mará says. Juan told me that Mará and her best friend Alina had joined the Yekîneyên Parastina Jin, YPJ, in Rojava in 2017 as internationalist fighters. On the 55th day of the resistance against the Turkish invasion of the small town of Afrîn, a bullet hit Mará in the right hip. A few days later, Alina died in a car accident in Hesekê, also in Rojava. Alina and Mará had met while studying Medicine in Havana and had gone to Syria together to support the Kurdish revolution.

Every cancer begins to grow at a specific point in the body and then, if remaining unnoticed, spreads uncontrollably and endlessly like the sea. Cancer knows no limit; indeed, it cancels out any sense of limitation.

Mará says that gardens allow people to accept the wild, the unfamiliar, the things they don't understand. "When you enter a garden, you enter another time. You'll never remember at what moment you entered; it is a time without a beginning or end, without a future." I ask Mará whether she has her own garden here in Buenos Aires. Pulling up her sunglasses, she looks at the bright red Shurei-mon. Her eyelashes are very short. She rubs her uncovered eyes, eyes that are glowing and glistening. Does she have hay fever or is she crying? How long has she been back?

"This is just a cliché. I've never been to Japan. But I've been reading a lot about Japanese gardens lately. Essentially, I guess it's about bringing human and cosmic space into contact with each other. Balance or harmony doesn't really play a big part in that, as far as I can see; it's about serenity and joy." Mará points to two large chunks of stone placed at a certain point on the lakeshore. I don't bother to ask why Mará is so interested in Japanese gardens. "Stones, for example, play a big role. The idea is that stones are neither dead nor silent. A stone grieves when it is unhappy. Stones should never just be placed superficially on the ground in gardens. They always have to be dug in a bit. In the tea garden, for instance, it's all about stones that you can't see. The stones in a garden are classified into three levels based on their significance: the main stones, the additional stones and the Oku stone. Oku has three meanings: 1. intimate, 2. sacred, and 3. covert. Oku is very often associated with Ma, which in Confucianism describes moments of silence, of the in-between. Ma is about the indeterminacy of boundaries; Oku is the indeterminacy of the centre. The Oku stone doesn't actually appear. Strictly speaking, it is not a stone at all. It is an idea: the undersurface of any appearance, an appearance that will never be fully visible—much like a half-buried stone. To me, that makes sense. The notion or thought that is yet unclear burrows itself to ripen in the darkness."

Juan's aunt entered the convent during the Argentinian military dictatorship. In the convent, no one was aware of her dual existence as a nun and underground resistance fighter. Her job was to pass on information to members of her unit. Juan's mother used to meet with her sister in parks or at the Buenos Aires Zoo. As inconspicuously as possible, always keeping their distance, they would leave crumpled pieces of paper with coded messages on the benches. When they left the meeting place again, for all the world, like Orpheus in the underworld, they were not allowed to turn around. Today, the aunt is within the protective scope of the mystic from Ávila: in the retirement home Residencial Santa Teresa de Cristo Rey.

I think, for Mará, it's about the idea of a place that contains the whole universe. But the Buenos Aires Japanese Gardens are actually less a garden than a park trying to convey an image of Japan that most who come here already are familiar with—a samurai, tea, cherry blossoms, origami, mochi, koi—mixed with Latin American flora. "Do you know the song *Hiroşima* by Zozan?" I know Zozan, but not the song. "She wrote it as a response to the Halabja poison gas attack. Hiroşima xuşka teye, bîra me dimîne." Mará sings the line; her voice is low.

Hiroshima is your sister; she will be kept in our memories. "I think Zozan should be invited to Japan on the next Hiroshima Memorial Day, and sing this song," Mará says.

My mother had untied the yellow plastic ribbon—over which she used to put wet laundry to dry—and hung it on the thickest branch of the pear tree. When she put the loop around her neck and pushed the chair away, the branch broke. She had only broken her arm. My father called me and I drove to the hospital. After her arm had been put in a cast, she was admitted to the psychiatric ward. There was a smoking room in the ward. An old woman was sitting in it, listening to the radio but not smoking. Daft Punk's *One More Time* was playing. My mother was in the hospital garden looking at a long row of low bushes with flowers the colour of blood oranges—a dark orange streaked with purple, haematoma-like patches. I approached her. She looked in my direction. I bent down to a blossom, consisting of countless fine, matchstick-like leaves. I blew, but it did not disperse. "The blossoms look like red dandelions, don't they?" Her voice broke frequently; the vocal cords were still pinched. "They're powder puff bushes."

How am I to imagine the day of decision? Alina and Mará, Argentine exchange students in Havana, after their anatomy course. It is the year 2016 according to our calendar. Just a moment ago they were exposing armpits of corpses. Now they are talking about the revolution and the *YPJ*. They are frustrated, have been for a long time. They want to engage in a meaningful, concrete form of resistance, not a theoretical one, not one oblivious of history. The revolution in Rojava needs women fighters and doctors. Women fighters: yes, for sure. Women doctors: even if they are still in training, their skills will certainly be sufficient for the revolution.

Everything that is alive can develop cancer.

I tell Mará about Jamaica Kincaid who writes that every garden is a reservoir of history, an exercise in memory; every garden produces stories that the gardener plants and creates in it. At the same time, says Kincaid, a garden evades the will of any gardener intending to control it. Mará points to the park with both her arms outstretched. "As I said, I've never been to Japan, but this mess here, this apparent denial of space, where things have been placed haphazardly, blocks the presence of the Oku stones meant to animate everything that doesn't reveal itself to the eye. Nothing can appear here."

I doubt the architects here cared about the principle of Oku stones, if they even knew of their existence. I would have liked to talk to Mará about her time in Rojava, but today's topic is Oku. If Mará is right, Oku means active disappearance. Oku is escaping from the world, not in order to ignore it, but because the world is something I must escape from. I disappear to escape representation.

My mother failed to herself. But her death wish had also failed to prepare her for the months of dying she was suddenly subjected to.

My favourite piece is *The Holy Presence of Joan D'Arc* for ten cellists by Julius Eastman. It lasts about twenty minutes. Eastman died of heart failure at Millard Fillmore Hospital in Buffalo on 28 May 1990, completely impoverished and homeless. As a composer and performer, Eastman had combined pop music and minimalism, classical and avant-garde from the 1960s onwards. At the time of his death, he had long since withdrawn from the public sphere. It was not until 22 January 1991, eight months after his death, that a journalist wrote an obituary for him.

Ecstasy can express itself in a scream, an uncontrolled movement, but likewise in quiet moments of contemplation when someone, like Mará, contemplates a scene from her past in front of the Shurei-mon at 33 degrees in the shade. The calm ecstasy of contemplation. "Hiroşima xuşka teye, bîra me dimîne," she sings.

I listen to Mará and think: music is merely a tool for communication with those who are no longer there. Music is always about absence. Disappearance becomes experience.

Hearing—so we can live with the absent. Listening—to survive them? Hearing in order to live. Listening to survive?

I know a wild garden by the sea. The gardener created it so he could die there. His garden was confined by nothing but the ocean. Though he had carefully chosen and laid out every element in his patch of soil, controlled chaos nonetheless prevailed there: uncertain, unfamiliar and unauthorized.

Jamaica Kincaid, who also writes: "I am in a state
of constant discomfort and I like this state so much
I would like to share it."
The garden begins with my body.

The text includes quotations and motifs from Jamaica
Kincaid's *My Garden (Book)* (Macmillan US, 1999), Sarah
Manguso's *Oceans* (The Paris Review, 228/2019), Jean-Luc
Nancy's *Listening* (Fordham University Press, 2007) and
Michel Tournier's *Gemini* (1997).

WENN ICH NUR ZU VERSCHWINDEN WÜSSTE

Mazlum Nergiz

Wenn ich nur zu verschwinden wüsste, gäbe es eine Vereinigung vollkommener Liebe zwischen Gott und der Erde, auf der ich gehe, und dem Meer, das ich höre.   Simone Weil

Der Japanische Garten von Buenos Aires liegt ungefähr 40 Minuten südöstlich vom trüben Río de la Plata entfernt. Ein Sonntag im Dezember. Der große, graue Himmel ist bedeckt von zerrissenen Wolken. Tief driften sie über der Stadt. Ein unklarer Wind treibt auch Mará und mich weg vom Río, der so breit ist, als habe er kein Ufer.
Ozeane sind ziellos. Flüsse nicht.
Mará ist eine alte Schulfreundin von Juan, meinem Ehemann. Beide sind in Berazategui aufgewachsen, einer kleinen Stadt im riesigen Einzugsgebiet von Buenos Aires. Während wir die Avenida Casares entlanglaufen, erzählt mir Mará, dass Berazategui die Hauptstadt des Glases sei. Hauptstadt des Glases? „Ja, die argentinische Glasindustrie hat sich schon früh dort angesiedelt. Warum, weiß ich auch nicht. Seit 1998 gibt es dort auch eine städtische Glasfachschule. Es ist die einzige in ganz Lateinamerika." Mará trägt ein zitronenfarbenes Tank-Top und sehr kurze Shorts. Lange, schwarze Haare, die glatt fallen. Ihre Flip-Flops schrammen über den Asphalt. Mará und ich haben uns vor zwei Stunden getroffen. Ihre Sonnenbrille hat sie seitdem noch nicht abgenommen.

Deswegen fällt es mir schwer, ihre Augen zu beschreiben. Was ich sehe: Dunkelbraune Sommersprossen. Ich sehe auch einige etwas hellere Flecke auf ihren spröden, vollen Lippen.
Seit meine Mutter versucht hat, sich in unserem Garten zu erhängen – und ich sie gemeinsam mit meinem Vater abbinden musste –, meide ich Gärten jeder Art. Leider verpasse ich während des Spaziergangs zum Japanischen Garten die Gelegenheit, den Besuch auf ein anderes Mal zu verschieben. Als wir vor dem Eingang des Jardín Japonés de la Ciudad de Buenos Aires stehen, schlage ich vor, dass wir lieber nach Berazategui fahren sollten. Mará lacht. „Was sollen wir in Berazategui?"
Juan ist mit seiner Schwester zu den Rindern gefahren, die sie vor zwei Jahren gekauft haben und um die sich eine Züchterin kümmert. Immer, wenn er in Argentinien ist, fahren die beiden für ein paar Tage zu den Rindern. Ich weiß nicht, was genau sie dort so lange machen. Ich habe Bilder von der Farm gesehen und mich entschieden, nicht mitzufahren.
Meine Mutter brachte mir bei, Cello zu spielen, als ich sieben Jahre alt war. Sie wollte mir das Zuhören beibringen. „Du musst spüren, wie der Ton sich ankündigt, kommt, vorübergeht, sich ausdehnt und durch dich hindurchdringt." Obwohl ich große Schwierigkeiten mit dem Notenlesen hatte, meinte ich zu verstehen, als sie mir erklärte, dass der Klang zwar sein Gesicht nicht verberge, sich aber auch nicht ertasten lasse: „Er ist ganz davor, dahinter und draußen, drinnen, drunter und drüber, überall, wie ein Geist." Mein Vater warf ihr vor, mir mit diesen Ausschweifungen das Instrument zu vergraulen, und wieso wir denn nicht einfach üben würden? Ich glaube, sie wollte mir erklären, dass es Räume gibt, die ich nicht sehen, nur hören kann.
Mará geht zur Kasse und kommt mit zwei blauen Papierscheinen zurück, die wie Getränkegutscheine aussehen. „Du kannst mit Juan

nach Berazategui fahren." Sie gibt mir mein Ticket und stellt sich in der kurzen Schlange an. Das grelle Licht der Sonne, das uns jetzt trifft, verwandelt Mará und die anderen wartenden Menschen in überbelichtete Schatten. Ich halte mein Ticket fest zwischen Daumen und Zeigefinger. Das Hupen der Autos löst sich in einem langen Ton auf. Mará kommt zurück und nimmt mich an der Hand, wie ein kleines Kind, das von unaufmerksamen Eltern vergessen wurde.

Nacht und Träume von Franz Schubert war das Lieblingsstück meiner Mutter. Ein Lied für eine Stimme und Klavier. Sie besorgte die Version für Klavier und Cello. Sie wollte, dass wir das Stück zusammen spielten. Ich sollte es mir selbst beibringen. Sie gab mir einen Monat Zeit. Dann wollte sie mich am Klavier dazu begleiten. Das Stück war viel zu schwierig für mich. An dem Tag, an dem das gemeinsame Musizieren hätte stattfinden sollen, kam meine Mutter früher als gewöhnlich nach Hause. Sie legte die Einkäufe auf den Tisch und rief meinen Vater an. Sie erzählte ihm, dass der Tumor in ihrer Brust so groß wäre, dass er bereits durch die Brustwand wuchs. Die Stunde fand trotzdem statt. Meine Mutter spielte am Klavier und ich hörte ihr zu. Vier Monate später ist sie gestorben. Einmal sagte meine Mutter: „Im Spielen musst du eine Verbindung mit dir selbst als Anderer herstellen." Was meinte sie? Redete sie von Ekstase? Musik als Versuch, meinen Körper zu überschreiten, ohne ihn zu verlassen?

In Mesopotamien wird der ekstatische Zustand mit maḫû beschrieben, außer sich, verrückt sein; rasen. In der griechischen Welt gibt es drei Begriffe für ihn: enthusiasmós, Gott in sich haben, manía, Wahnsinn, und später ékstasis, außer sich sein. Das alte Rom kennt kaum Begriffe für Ekstase. Schon die Terminologie ist abwertend: furor. Die offizielle christliche Lehre weiß auch von nichts, außer Ekstatikerinnen werden im Neuen Testament und in den Heiligenlegenden als von Dämonen besessen geheilt. Aber wir kennen, zum Beispiel, die berühmte Mystikerin Teresa aus Ávila, wo in einem der Klöster ein Teil ihres verrottenden Mittelfingers zu sehen ist. Teresa, deren Herz von einem Engel, der ihr erschien, durchbohrt wurde. Als ihr Körper 1582 exhumiert wurde, fand man dieses wohl vollständig intakt vor. Es wurde entfernt, und dann meinte man, eine wirkliche Wunde im Herzen zu sehen, verursacht durch den Speer des Engels. Heute liegt ihr Herz in einer goldenen Schatulle im Convento de la Anunciación in Alba de Tormes.

Was ich vergessen habe, sie zu fragen: Wo ist dieser Andere meines Selbst, wenn ich gerade nicht zuhöre?

Der Jardín Japonés ist um einen See herum angelegt. Unförmige, sich wahnsinnig verrenkende Florettseidenbäume mit pinken Blütenblättern säumen den Weg. Ihre Rinden sind von Stacheln durchbohrt. Sie wechseln sich ab mit eleganten Tipubäumen, deren Äste sich weit ausdehnen. Gefiederte Blätter, strahlend gelbe Blüten. Im See liegt eine kleine Insel, die mit medizinischen Kräutern aus Japan bepflanzt worden ist. Zwei kurze Brücken führen zu ihr. Wir kommen an einer miniaturhaften Nachbildung des Shurei-mon vorbei. Mará setzt sich auf einen Steinsockel gegenüber der Kopie des berühmten Eingangstors auf Okinawa, das einen zur Burg Shuri führt. Vier Säulen tragen die zwei übereinander gelegten Dächer. Das rechte Bein tue ihr weh, sagt Mará. Juan hat mir erzählt, dass Mará und ihre beste Freundin Alina sich 2017 als internationalistische Kämpferinnen der Yekîneyên Parastina Jin, YPJ, in Rojava angeschlossen hatten. Am 55. Tag des Widerstands gegen die türkische Invasion der Kleinstadt Afrîn traf Mará eine Kugel in die rechte Hüfte. Ein paar Tage später ist Alina bei einem Autounfall in Hesekê, ebenfalls in Rojava, ums Leben gekommen. Alina und Mará hatten sich beim Medizinstudium in Havanna kennengelernt und waren zusammen nach Syrien gegangen, um die kurdische Revolution zu unterstützen.

Jeder Krebs beginnt an einem spezifischen Punkt im Körper zu wachsen, um sich dann, falls er unbemerkt bleibt, unkontrolliert und endlos wie das Meer auszubreiten. Krebs kennt keine Grenze, hebt vielmehr jedes Verständnis von Begrenzung auf.

Mará sagt, dass Gärten den Menschen ermöglichen, das Wilde, das Fremde, das, was sie nicht verstehen, zu akzeptieren. „Wenn du einen Garten betrittst, betrittst du eine andere Zeit. Du wirst dich niemals an den Moment des Eintritts erinnern, es ist eine Zeit ohne Anfang und Ende, ohne Zukunft." Ich frage Mará, ob sie hier in Buenos Aires denn einen eigenen Garten habe. Sie zieht ihre Sonnenbrille hoch und betrachtet das knallrot lackierte Shureimon. Ihre Wimpern sind sehr kurz. Sie reibt sich die entblößten Augen, die glühen und glitzern. Hat sie Heuschnupfen oder weint sie? Wie lange ist sie schon wieder zurück?

„Das hier ist nur ein Klischee. Ich war noch nie in Japan. Aber in letzter Zeit lese ich viel über japanische Gärten. Grundsätzlich, glaube ich, geht es darum, den menschlichen und den kosmischen Raum miteinander in Berührung zu bringen. Dabei spielt Gleichgewicht oder Harmonie, soweit ich es überblicke, nicht wirklich eine große Rolle, sondern Heiterkeit und Freude." Mará zeigt auf zwei große Brocken, die an einer Stelle des Seeufers platziert worden sind. Ich frage nicht nach, warum Mará sich so sehr für japanische Gärten interessiert. „Steine zum Beispiel spielen eine große Rolle. Es geht darum, dass Steine weder tot noch stumm sind. Ein Stein klagt, wenn er unglücklich ist. Steine dürfen in Gärten nie einfach nur auf den Boden gelegt werden. Sie müssen immer ein kleines bisschen eingegraben sein. Im Teegarten zum Beispiel geht es um Steine, die man nicht sieht. Die Steine in einem Garten werden ihrer Bedeutung nach in drei Stufen eingeteilt: die Hauptsteine, die Zusatzsteine und der Oku-Stein. Oku hat drei Bedeutungen: 1. intim, 2. heilig, und 3. verborgen. Oku wird sehr oft mit Ma in Verbindung gebracht, das im Konfuzianismus Momente der Stille, des Dazwischen beschreibt. Ma dreht sich um die Unbestimmtheit der Grenzen, Oku ist die Unbestimmtheit des Zentrums. Der Oku-Stein tritt nicht in Erscheinung. Strikt gesprochen ist er überhaupt kein Stein. Er ist eine Idee; die Unterseite jeder Erscheinung; eine Erscheinung, die niemals völlig sichtbar sein wird, genauso wie ein halb eingegrabener Stein. Ich finde, das macht Sinn. Der Gedanke, der noch unklar ist, gräbt sich ein, um in der Dunkelheit reif zu werden."

Juans Tante trat während der argentinischen Militärdiktatur ins Kloster ein. Im Kloster wusste niemand von ihrer Doppelexistenz als Nonne und Widerstandskämpferin im Untergrund. Ihre Aufgabe war es, Informationen an Mitglieder ihrer Zelle weiterzuleiten. Juans Mutter traf sich mit ihrer Schwester in Parks oder im Zoo von Buenos Aires. So unauffällig wie möglich, immer die Distanz wahrend, ließen sie zerknüllte Zettel mit verschlüsselten Nachrichten auf den Sitzbänken zurück. Wenn sie den Treffpunkt wieder verließen, durften sie sich, um alles in der Welt, wie Orpheus in der Unterwelt, nicht umdrehen. Heute liegt die Tante im Schutzbereich der Mystikerin aus Ávila: im Seniorenheim Residencial Santa Teresa de Cristo Rey.

Ich glaube, Mará geht es um die Idee eines Orts, in dem das ganze Universum enthalten ist. Aber der Japanische Garten von Buenos Aires ist weniger Garten als Parkanlage, die versucht, ein Bild von Japan zu vermitteln, das die meisten, die hierherkommen, bereits kennen – Samurai, Tee, Kirschblüten, Origami, Mochi, Kois, vermischt mit lateinamerikanischer Flora. „Kennst du das Lied *Hiroşima* von Zozan?" Ich kenne Zozan, aber nicht das Lied. „Sie hat es in Reaktion auf den Giftgasangriff von Halabja geschrieben. Hiroşima xuşka teye, bîra me dimîne." Mará singt die Zeile. Ihre Stimme ist tief.

Hiroshima ist deine Schwester, sie wird uns in

Erinnerung bleiben. „Ich finde, Zozan sollte beim nächsten Hiroshima-Gedenktag nach Japan eingeladen werden und dieses Lied singen", sagt Mará.

Meine Mutter hatte das gelbe Plastikband, über das sie die nasse Wäsche zum Trocknen legte, abgebunden und es an den dicksten Ast des Birnbaums gehangen. Als sie die Schlaufe um ihren Hals legte und den Stuhl wegstieß, brach der Ast ab. Sie hatte sich nur den Arm gebrochen. Mein Vater rief mich an und ich fuhr ins Krankenhaus. Nachdem ihr Arm eingegipst worden war, wurde sie in die Psychiatrie eingewiesen. Auf der Station gab es einen Raucherraum. Eine alte Frau saß darin. Sie hörte Radio, rauchte aber nicht. Es lief Daft Punks *One More Time*. Meine Mutter war im Garten der Klinik und betrachtete eine lange Reihe von tiefen Sträuchern mit Blüten, die die Farbe von Blutorangen hatten – ein dunkles Orange, das von violetten, hämatomhaften Flecken durchzogen war. Ich näherte mich ihr. Sie blickte zu mir. Ich beugte mich herunter zu einer Blüte. Sie bestand aus unzähligen feinen, streichholzartigen Blättern. Ich blies, doch sie löste sich nicht auf. „Die Blüten sehen aus wie rote Pusteblumen, oder?" Ihre Stimme brach sehr oft. Die Stimmbänder waren noch eingeklemmt. „Das sind Puderquastensträucher."

Wie muss ich mir den Tag der Entscheidung vorstellen? Alina und Mará, argentinische Austauschstudentinnen in Havanna, nach ihrem Präparationskurs. Es ist das Jahr 2016 nach unserer Zeitrechnung. Gerade haben sie noch die Achseln freigelegt. Jetzt sprechen sie über die Revolution und die YPJ. Sie sind frustriert, lange schon. Sie wollen einen sinnvollen, konkreten Widerstand leisten, keinen theoretischen, keinen geschichtsvergessenen. Die Revolution in Rojava braucht Kämpferinnen und Ärztinnen. Kämpferinnen: ja, auf jeden Fall. Ärztinnen: sie befinden sich zwar noch in Ausbildung, aber für die Revolution reicht es sicherlich.

Alles, was lebt, kann Krebs entwickeln.

Ich erzähle Mará von Jamaica Kincaid, die schreibt, dass jeder Garten ein Speicher für Geschichte, „an exercise in memory", eine Übung in Erinnerung, ist. Jeder Garten bringt Geschichten hervor, die die Gärtnerin in ihm einpflanzt und anlegt. Gleichzeitig, sagt Kincaid, entzieht sich der Garten dem Willen der Gärtnerin, die ihn kontrollieren will. Mará zeigt mit ihren beiden ausgestreckten Armen auf die Parkanlage. „Wie gesagt, ich war noch nie in Japan, aber dieses Durcheinander hier, dieses offensichtliche Leugnen des Raumes, in dem Dinge willkürlich platziert werden, blockiert die Präsenz der Oku-Steine, die alles beleben, was sich dem Auge nicht zeigt. Hier kann nichts erscheinen."

Ich bezweifle, dass die Architekten hier sich um das Prinzip der Oku-Steine gekümmert haben, wenn sie denn überhaupt von ihrer Existenz wussten. Ich hätte gerne mit Mará über ihre Zeit in Rojava gesprochen, aber heute geht es um Oku. Wenn Mará Recht hat, ist Oku aktives Verschwinden. Oku ist die Flucht aus der Welt, nicht um sie zu ignorieren, sondern weil die Welt etwas ist, vor der ich fliehen muss. Ich verschwinde, um der Darstellung zu entkommen.

Meine Mutter hat es nicht geschafft, sich selber umzubringen. Doch ihre Todessehnsucht hat sie nicht auf das monatelange Sterben vorbereitet, dem sie plötzlich ausgeliefert war.

Mein Lieblingsstück ist *The Holy Presence of Joan D'Arc* für zehn Cellisten von Julius Eastman. Es dauert ungefähr zwanzig Minuten. Eastman starb am 28. Mai 1990 völlig verarmt und obdachlos im Millard Fillmore Hospital in Buffalo an Herzversagen. Als Komponist und Performer verknüpfte Eastman ab den 1960er Jahren Popmusik und Minimalismus, Klassik und Avantgarde miteinander. Zum Zeitpunkt seines Todes hatte er sich schon lange aus der Öffentlichkeit zurückgezogen. Erst am 22. Januar 1991, acht Monate nach seinem Tod, verfasste ein Journalist einen Nachruf auf ihn.

23 Ekstase kann sich in einem Schrei, einer unkontrollier-
ten Bewegung, aber auch in ruhigen Momenten der Kontemplation ausdrücken, wenn jemand, wie zum Beispiel
Margá vor dem Shurei-mon bei 33 Grad im Schatten eine
Szene aus ihrer Vergangenheit betrachtet. Ruhige Eks-
tase der Kontemplation. „Hiroşima xuşka teye, bîra me
dimîne", singt sie.
Ich höre Margá zu und denke: Musik ist nur ein
Behelfsmittel, um mit denen zu kommunizieren, die nicht mehr da sind. Es geht in der Musik
immer um Abwesenheit. Das Verschwinden wird
zu Erfahrung.
Hören, um mit den Abwesenden zu leben. Zuhören, um
sie zu überleben?
Hören, um zu leben. Zuhören, um zu überleben?
Ich kenne einen wilden Garten am Meer. Der
Gärtner hat ihn angelegt, um dort zu sterben.
Sein Garten wurde von nichts begrenzt außer
vom Ozean. Er hatte zwar jedes Element in
seinem Gartenstück sorgfältig ausgesucht und
angelegt, doch trotzdem herrschte kontrollier-
tes Chaos: unsicher, fremd und unautorisiert.
Jamaica Kincaid, die auch schreibt: „I am in a state of
constant discomfort and I like this state so much I would
like to share it."
Der Garten beginnt mit meinem Körper.

Der Text verwendet Zitate und Motive aus Jamaica Kin-
caids *My Garden (Book)* (Macmillan US, 1999), Sarah Man-
gusos *Oceans* (The Paris Review, Ausgabe 228/2019) Jean-
Luc Nancys *Zum Gehör* (Diaphanes, 2002) und Michel
Tourniers *Zwillingssterne* (Fischer, 1975).

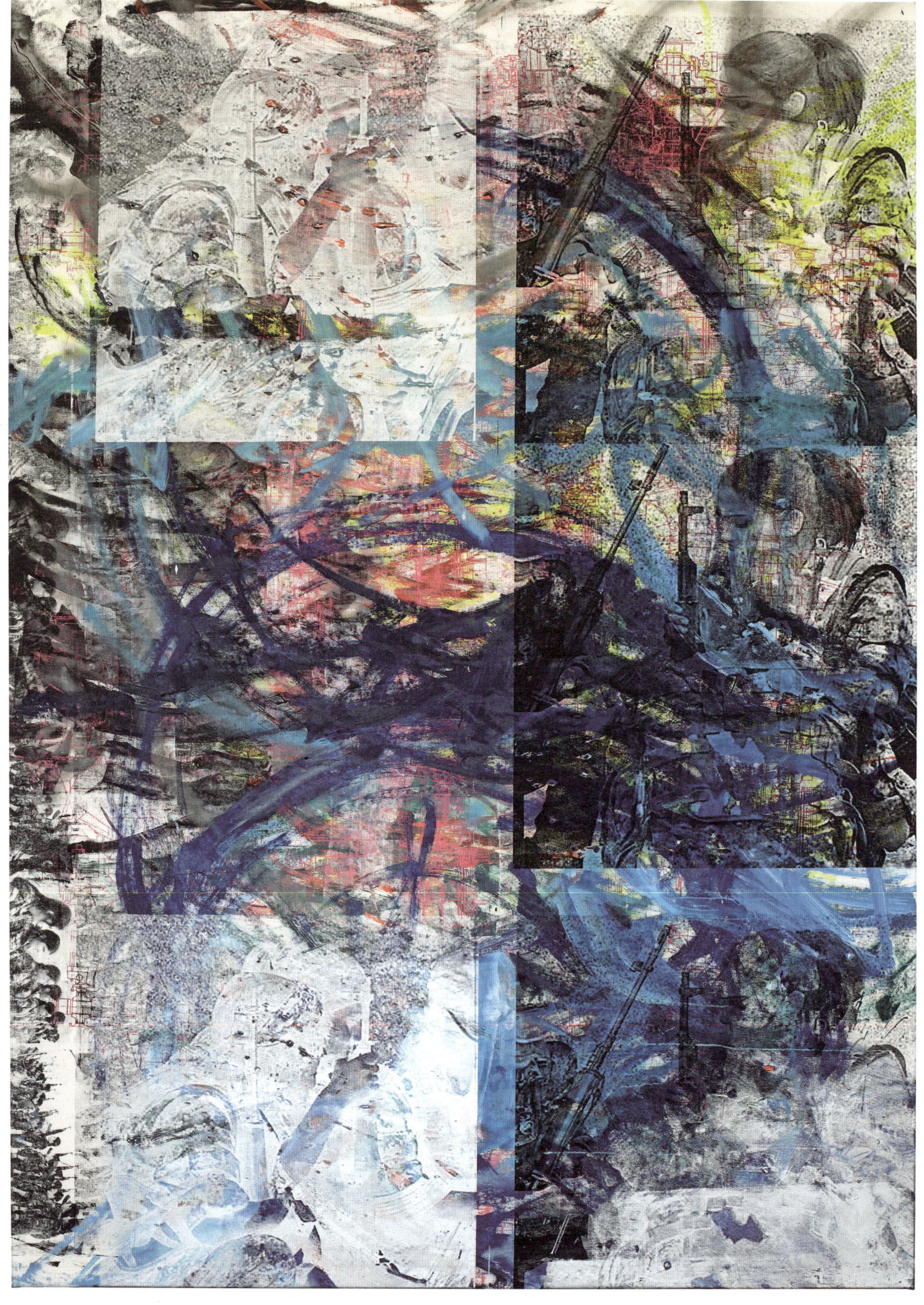

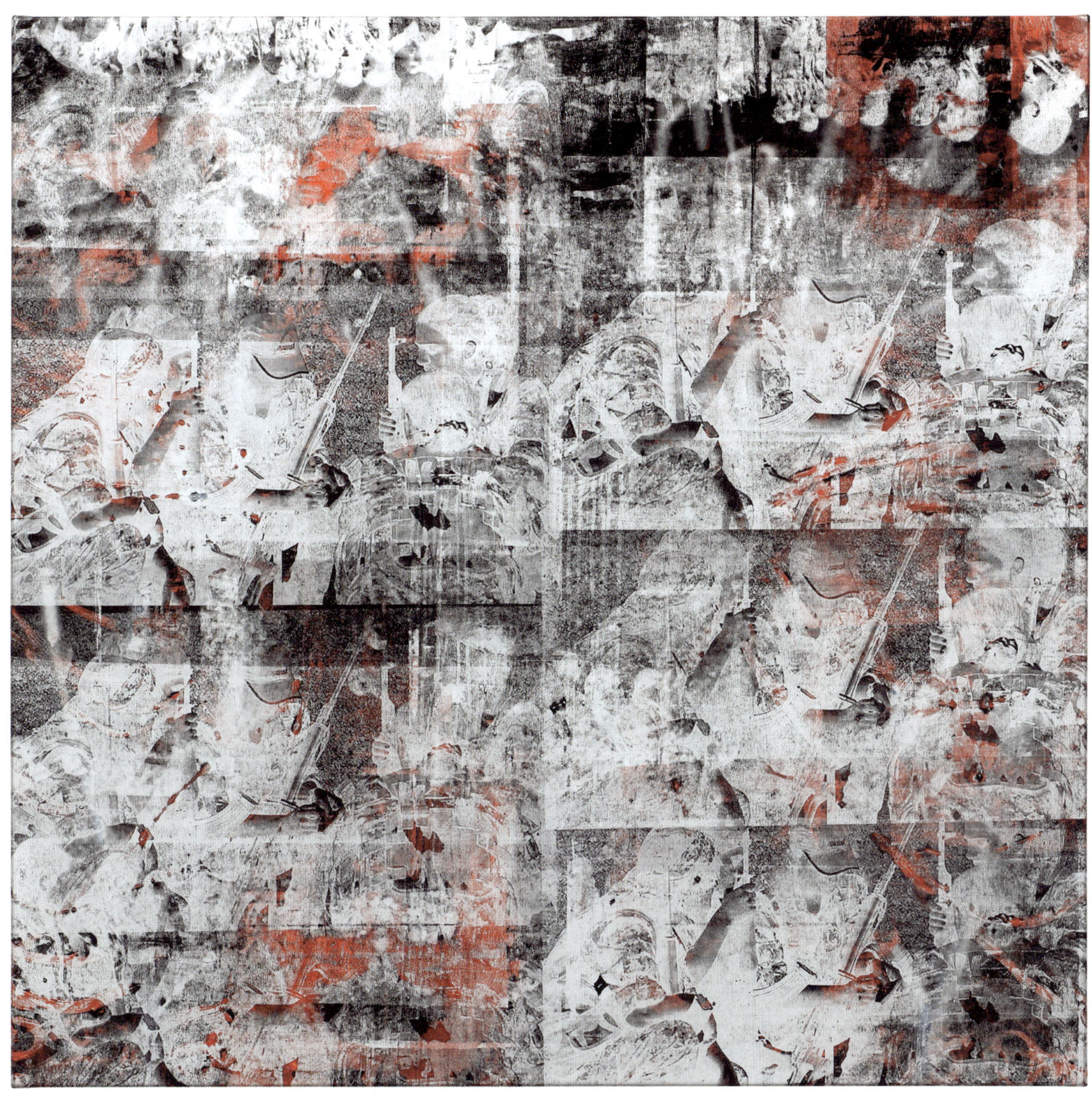

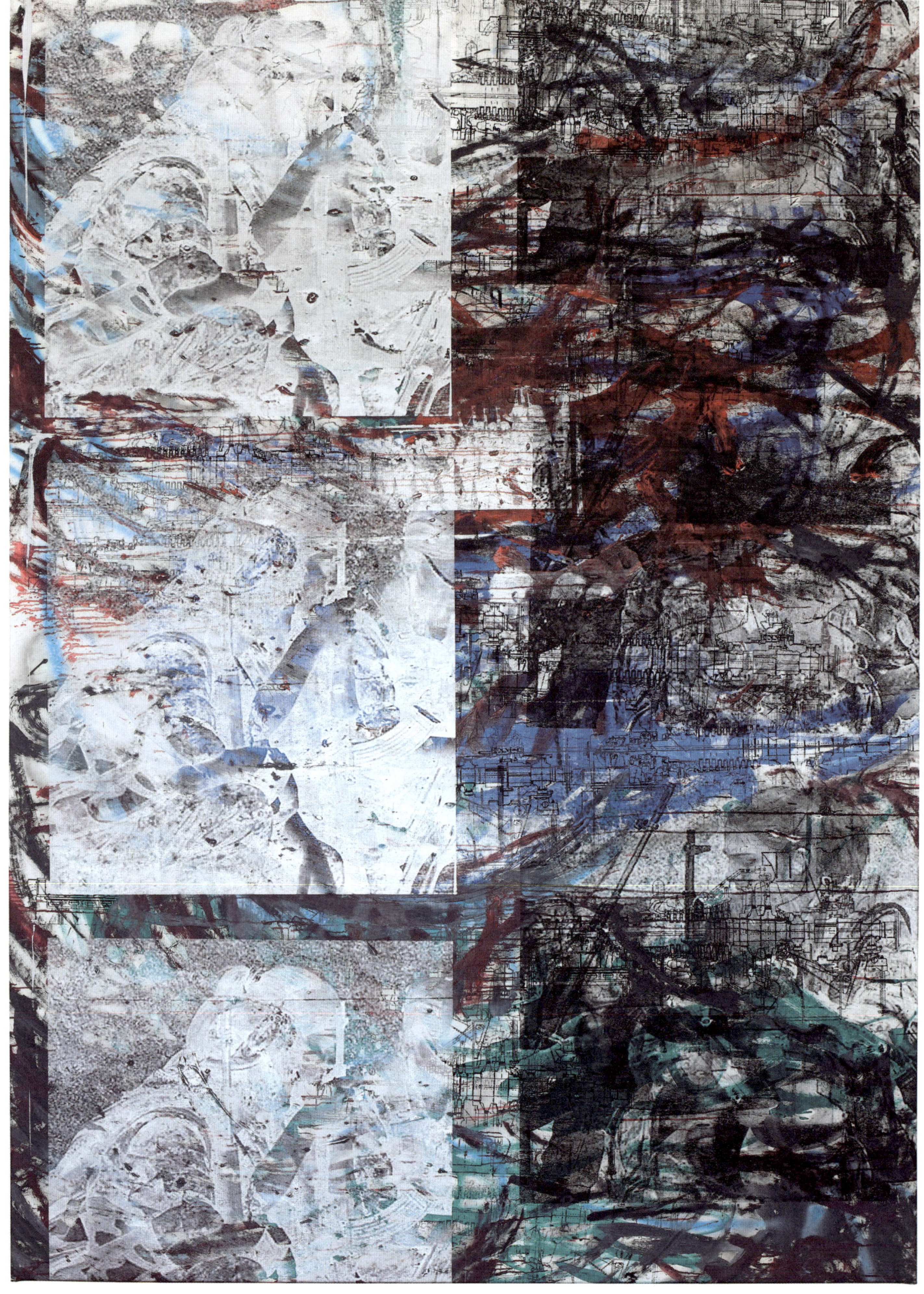

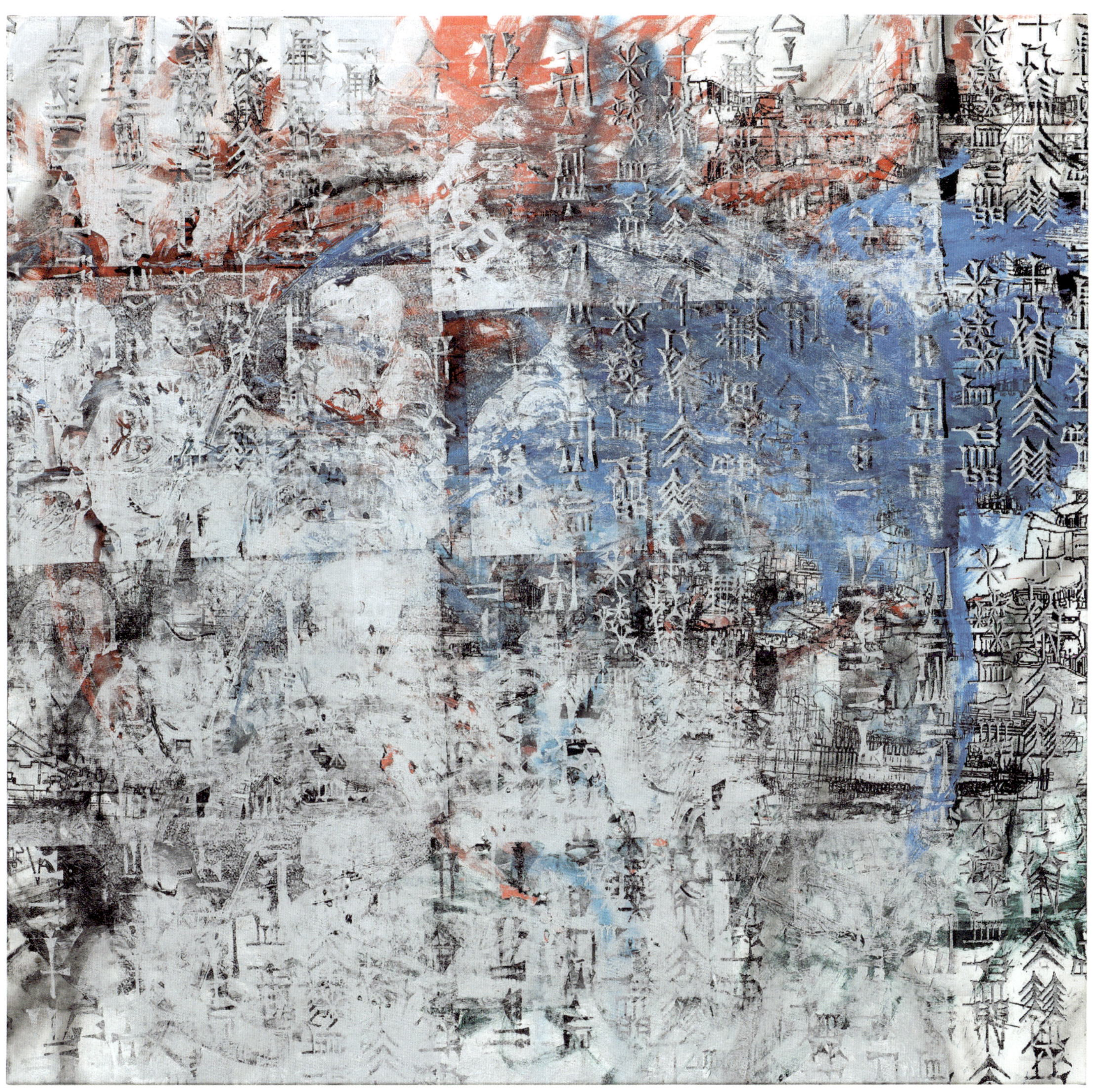

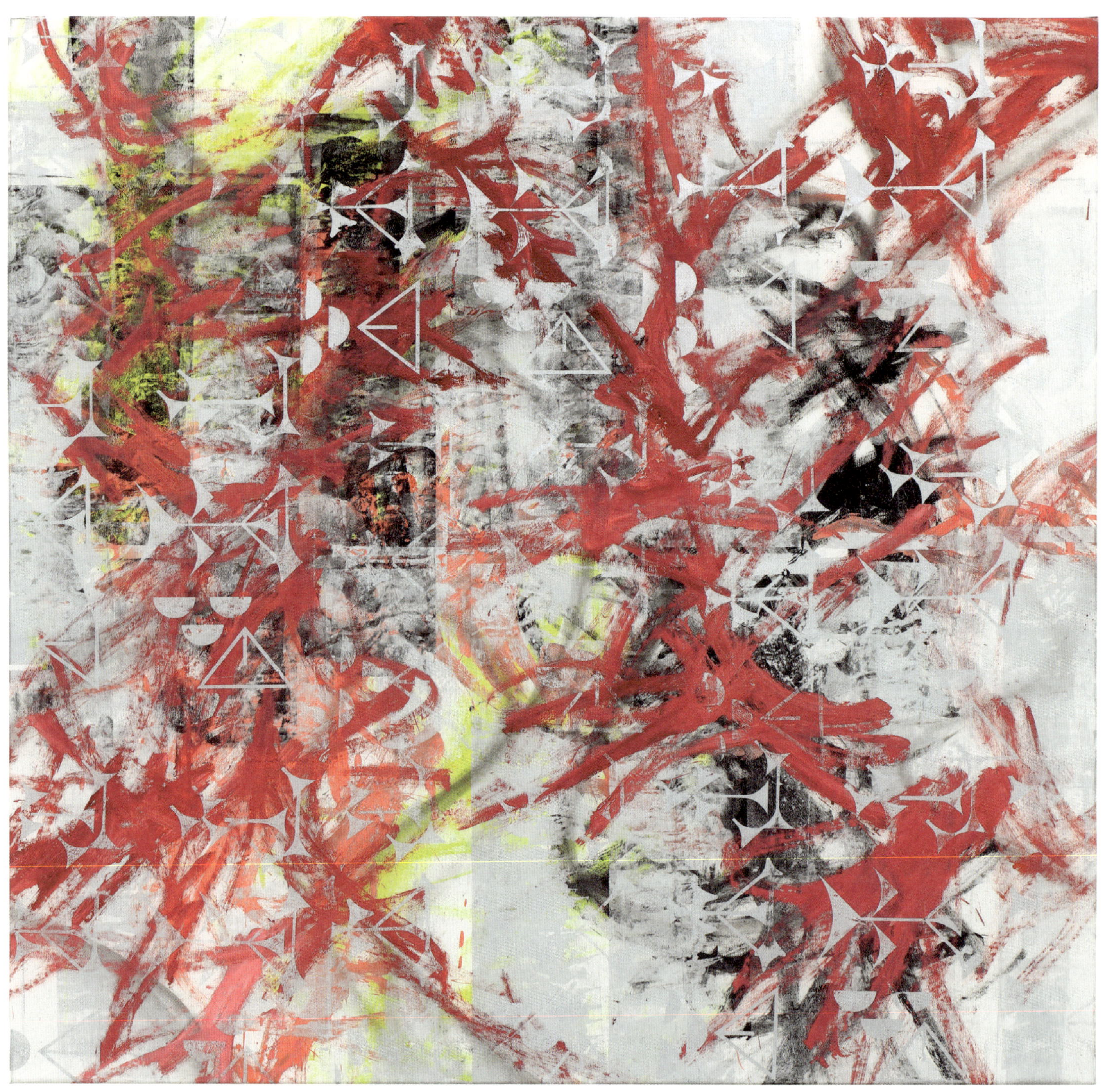

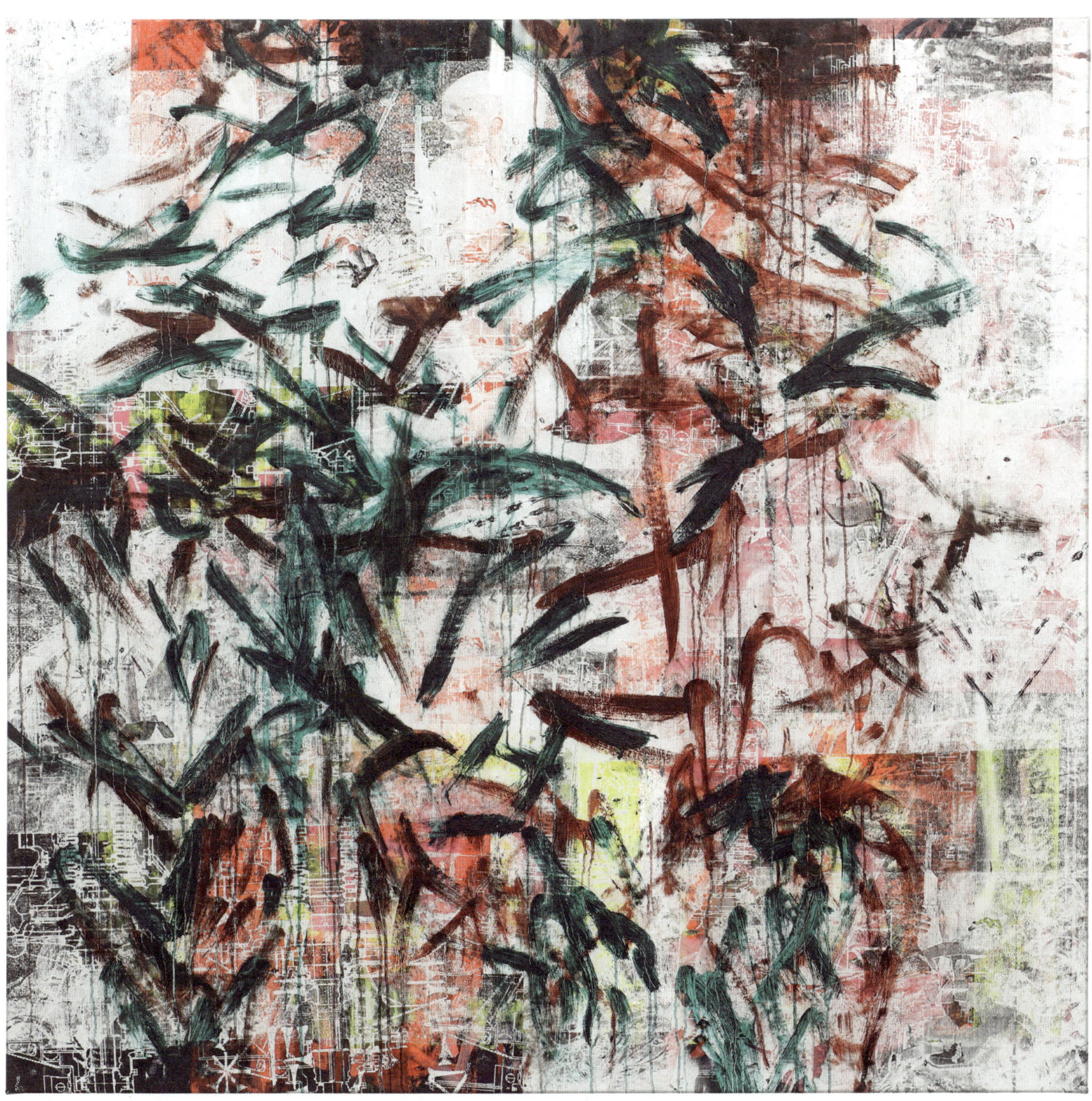

WHAT I THINK OF WHEN
I THINK OF LEYLA'S WORKS

Enis Maci

1

The way she lies in bed, an anime-like cloud castle of
pillows behind her back. How she reads Proust.

Swann, living his life.

2

Of a cemetery on an island in the midst of a reservoir.

The island once was a hill. And at its feet: a village. It was flooded,
making sure there would be nothing left of those who lived there.

The dead reburied on the hilltop, no: all the dead are a trace.
Leyla follows it.

Rushing traffic outside my window. I think of the volcano peaks we call
islands or mountains, sparkling harmlessly in the morning light.

What does a name change?

3

Can it be done: questioning the fabrication of things,
while you yourself produce, fabricate? Questioning
the extraction of the visible from the concealed, while you
yourself extract, distillate?

4

Of the eeriness underlying second-hand experiences. Annihilation—
and life, blindly attacking it.

Under intense heat, fusing what's already there. Releasing the ore from
the stone. Sweaty Hephaistos, feisty Kawa, and Pele who eats earth and
is earth—I suppose these could be the patron saints of Leyla's work.

5

Of my asshole, inevitably contracting with every boom.
A bass that grabs you by the guts. Right here—it pulls you
out, out of yourself, out of your skin, into the open.

6

Of DIKKE BLEECH that kills off all dirt. I think of: ACE, purchased
in the corner shop of the Indian family that later had to concede in
the neighbourly price war, due to the competition's start-up attitude.
And: ACID PËR WC, import into the European Union prohibited.

Dead fish, adorning red plastic.

7

So I think of cleaning, picking, tinkering, soldering, forging.

Hi Fi DIY.

I don't think about genres.

There is only the work which is a connecting and dismem-
bering work. Something beautiful, if beauty means ripping
the wings out of a frozen chicken. If beauty means
nourishing somebody else.

To be divisible by nothing, except oneself.

8

Rosaceae is the Latin name of the rose family.

Agamben writes that English is not at all comparable to Latin because
English is the language of an existent empire, whereas Latin only
became the true *lingua franca* when the Roman Empire was no more.

9

Of the English plumber Anna Campbell, who fell as Hêlîn
Qereçox.

At the empires' margins, for the sake of a world without
empires: for life.

10

Of a creaking like celluloid that creeps over a reel. That becomes foot-
steps. Gravel crunching under Helbest's feet.

11

And Proust again, or rather Leyla reading Proust:
"At Combray, where I knew everyone, and could always
detect the blacksmith or grocer's boy through his disguise
of a beadle's uniform or chorister's surplice, this fisherman
was the only person whom I was never able to identify."

12

Of eyes closing and opening; a small, merciful sun flitting through the
curtains. Of girls laughing.

Being relaxed. Barely breathing; unable to calm down, out of sheer joy.

13

Of a grey that is actually a grainy khaki, concerning
the old films.

Khaki like a military uniform or the gardener's smock
apron at Combray, the gardener who is actually a blacksmith, or a grocer's boy.

"actually"

14

Nocturnal ink from which the landscape crystallizes.
Cave paintings without a cave.

Reversed snowmelt: white floes growing from blackness.

Anime clouds, being at home.

15

Of cuneiform writing.

To imprint oneself in the still damp sound, which can be a hum or a
sustained scream that turns out to be the sound of a defective escalator,
at the train station, at half past three in the morning.

It's been years since I came here at this hour. There's a solitary man
waiting under the neon lights of the reception centre. The advertising
shifts as I walk past. The animal roar of a regional express. The escalator
screeches like untuned violins in an orchestra pit, only that no
audience shows up.

16

Watch out, Beritan, neighs the horse.

Its name is not Falada.

Its head does not adorn a castle gate.

It crosses all paths, and lives.

WORAN ICH DENKE, WENN ICH AN LEYLAS ARBEITEN DENKE

Enis Maci

1

Wie sie im Bett liegt, ein animemäßiges
Wolkenschloss aus Kissen hinter ihrem
Rücken. Wie sie Proust liest.

Swann, der sein Leben lebt.

2

An einen Friedhof auf einer Insel in der Mitte eines
Stausees.

Die Insel ist einmal ein Hügel gewesen. Und zu seinen
Füßen: ein Dorf. Es wurde geflutet, damit da nichts
mehr sei, von denen, die da lebten.

Die auf die Hügelkuppe umgebetteten Toten, nein: Alle
Toten sind eine Spur. Leyla folgt ihr.

Vor meinem Fenster rauscht der Verkehr. Ich denke an
die harmlos im Morgenlicht funkelnden Spitzen der
Vulkane, die wir Inseln nennen oder Berge.

Was ändert ein Name?

3

Andere Frage:
Geht das denn – selbst herstellend, das Herstellen selbst in Frage stellen, das Extrahie-
ren des Sichtbaren aus dem Verborgenen?

4

Ans Gespenstische, das in den Erfahrungen zweiter
Hand liegt. Die Vernichtung und das sie blindlings
attackierende Leben.

Unter großer Hitze verbinden, was ohnehin schon da
ist. Das Erz aus dem Stein lösen. Sweaty Hephaistos,
feisty Kawa, und Pele, die Erde frisst und Erde ist –
ich glaube, das könnten die Schutzheiligen von Leylas
Arbeit sein.

5

An mein Arschloch, das sich bei jedem Dröh-
nen unwillkürlich zusammenzieht. Bass, der
in die Eingeweide greift. Hier – ziehts dich
raus, aus dir, aus deiner Haut – ins Freie.

6

An DIKKE BLEECH, die jedem Dreck den Garaus
macht. An: ACE, im Büdchen jener indischen Familie
gekauft, die später im nachbarschaftlichen Prelskampf
kapitulieren musste, der Start Up-Attitüde der
Konkurrenz wegen. Und: ACID PËR WC, Einfuhr in
die Europäische Union verboten.

Tote Fische, die rotes Plastik zieren.

7

Ich denke also ans Putzen, Pulen, Frickeln,
Löten, Schmieden.

Hi Fi DIY.

Ich denke nicht an Genres.

Es gibt nur die Arbeit, die eine Verbindungs-
und Zerstückelungsarbeit ist. Etwas

Schönes, wenn Schönheit heißt, einem
tiefgefrorenen Huhn die Flügel rauszurei-
ßen. Wenn Schönheit heißt, einen anderen
zu nähren.

Durch nichts teilbar sein, außer durch sich.

8
Rosaceae ist der lateinische Name der Rosengewächse.

Agamben schreibt, das Englische sei überhaupt
nicht mit dem Lateinischen vergleichbar, weil
das Englische die Sprache eines noch existierenden
Imperiums sei, das Lateinische aber erst dann zur
wahren Lingua franca wurde, als das Römische Reich
nicht mehr war.

9
An die englische Klempnerin Anna Campbell, die als Hêlîn Qereçox fiel.

An den Rändern der Reiche, um einer Welt
ohne Reiche willen: für das Leben.

10
An ein Knistern wie Zelluloid, das über eine Spule
kriecht. Das zu Schritten wird. Kies, der unter Helbests
Füßen knirscht.

11
Und wieder Proust, oder Leyla, die Proust
liest:
„In Combray, wo ich den Schmied oder
Ladenjungen stets hinter der Verkleidung
einer Gärtneruniform oder eines Chor-
hemds zu erkennen vermochte, blieb dieser

Fischer die einzige Person, deren Identität
ich niemals aufdeckte."

12
An Augen, die sich schließen und öffnen; an eine kleine,
barmherzige Sonne, die durch die Gardinen huscht.
An Mädchen, die lachen.

Gelöst sein. Kaum mehr atmen; sich vor Freude nicht
beruhigen können.

13
An ein Grau, das eigentlich ein körniges
Khaki ist, die alten Filme betreffend.

Khaki wie eine Militäruniform oder die
Kittelschürze des Gärtners in Combray,
des Gärtners, der eigentlich ein Schmied
ist, oder ein Ladenjunge.

„eigentlich"

14
Nächterne Tinte, aus der sich die Landschaft schält.
Höhlenmalereien ohne Höhle.

Umgekehrte Schneeschmelze: weiße Schollen, die aus
Schwärze wachsen.

Animewolken, Zuhausesein.

15
An die Keilschrift.

Sich einprägen in den noch feuchten Ton,
der ein Summen sein kann oder ein

langgezogener Schrei, der sich als das
Geräusch einer defekten Rolltreppe
entpuppt, morgens um halb vier
am Bahnhof.

Seit Jahren war ich nicht zu dieser Urzeit
dort. Ein einzelner Mann wartet unter der
Neonröhre des Aufnahmezentrums.
Die Werbung bewegt sich, wenn ich
vorbeilaufe. Das tierische Röhren eines
Regionalexpress. Die Rolltreppe quietscht
wie ungestimmte Geigen im Orchestergra-
ben, nur kommt kein Publikum.

16
Pass auf, Beritan, wiehert das Pferd.

Es heißt nicht Falada.

Sein Haupt ziert kein Burgtor.

Es quert alle Wege, und lebt.

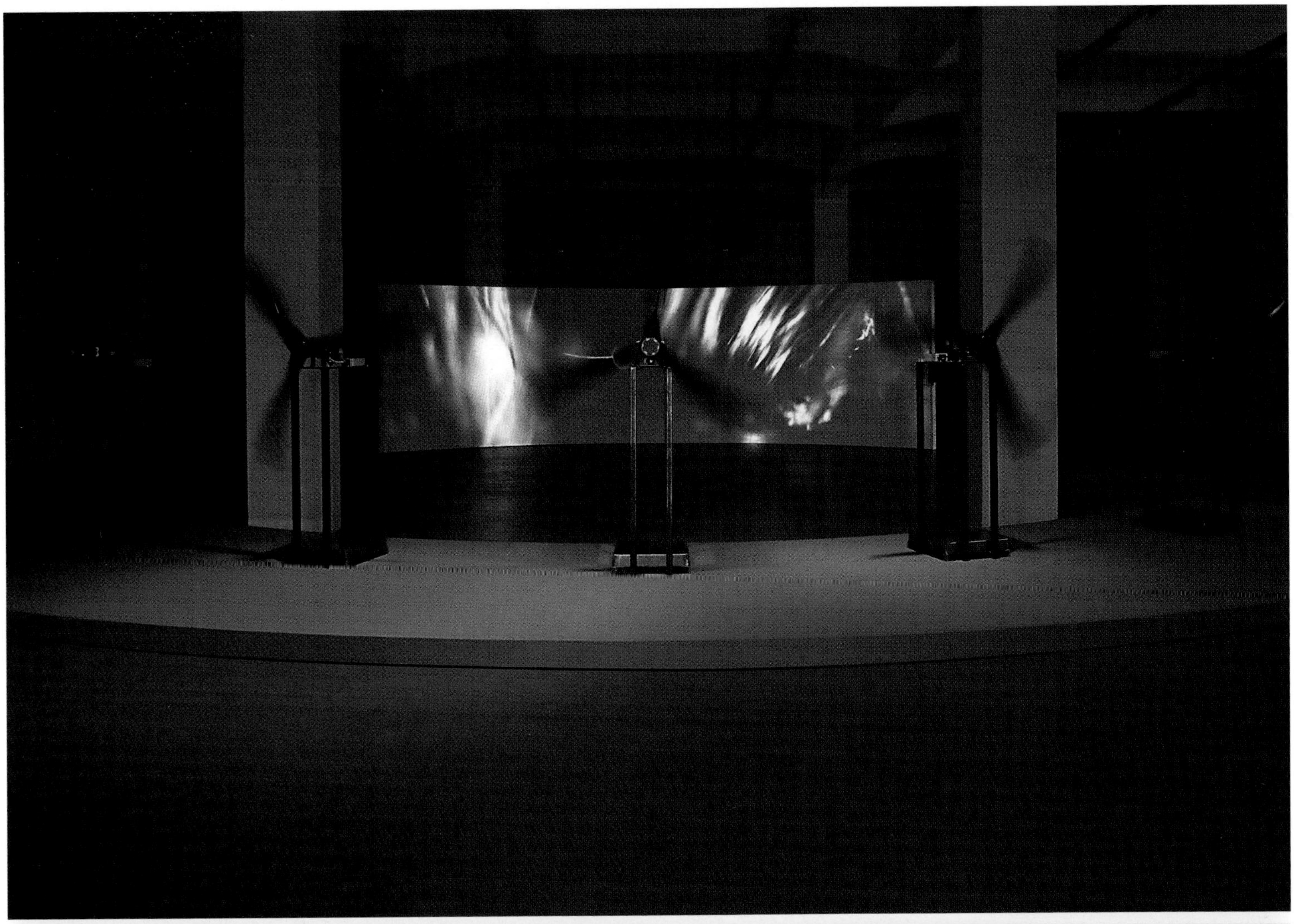

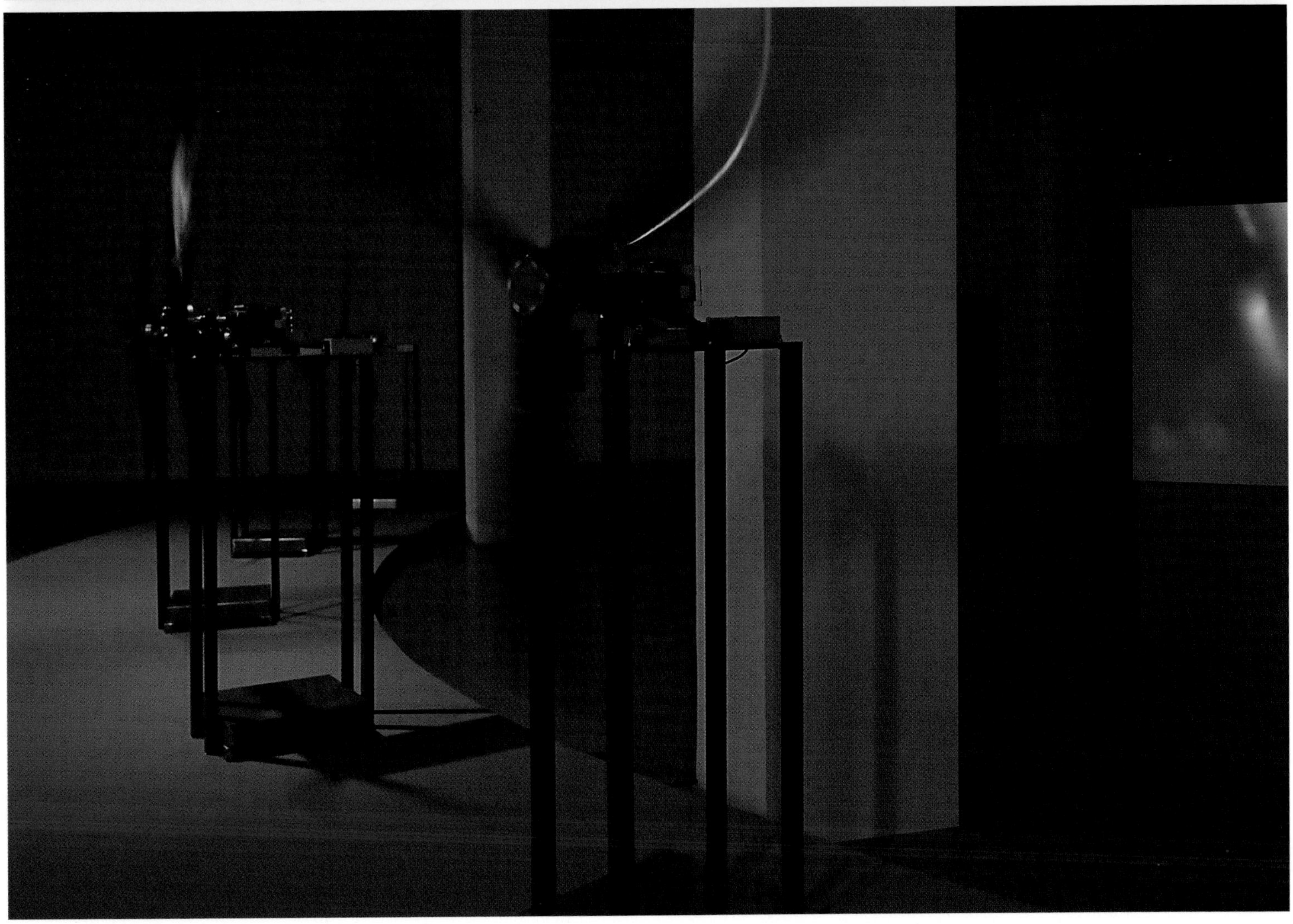

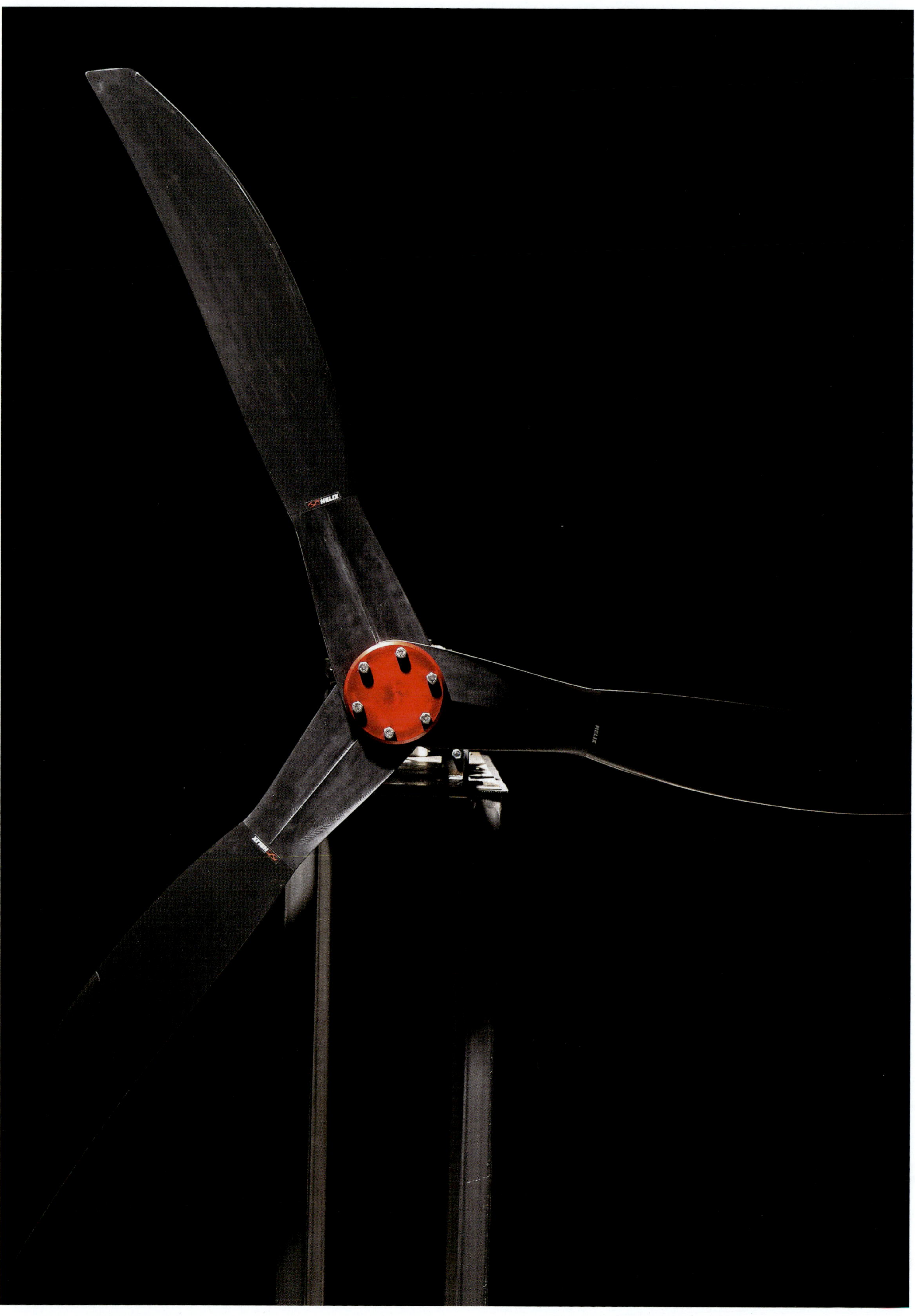

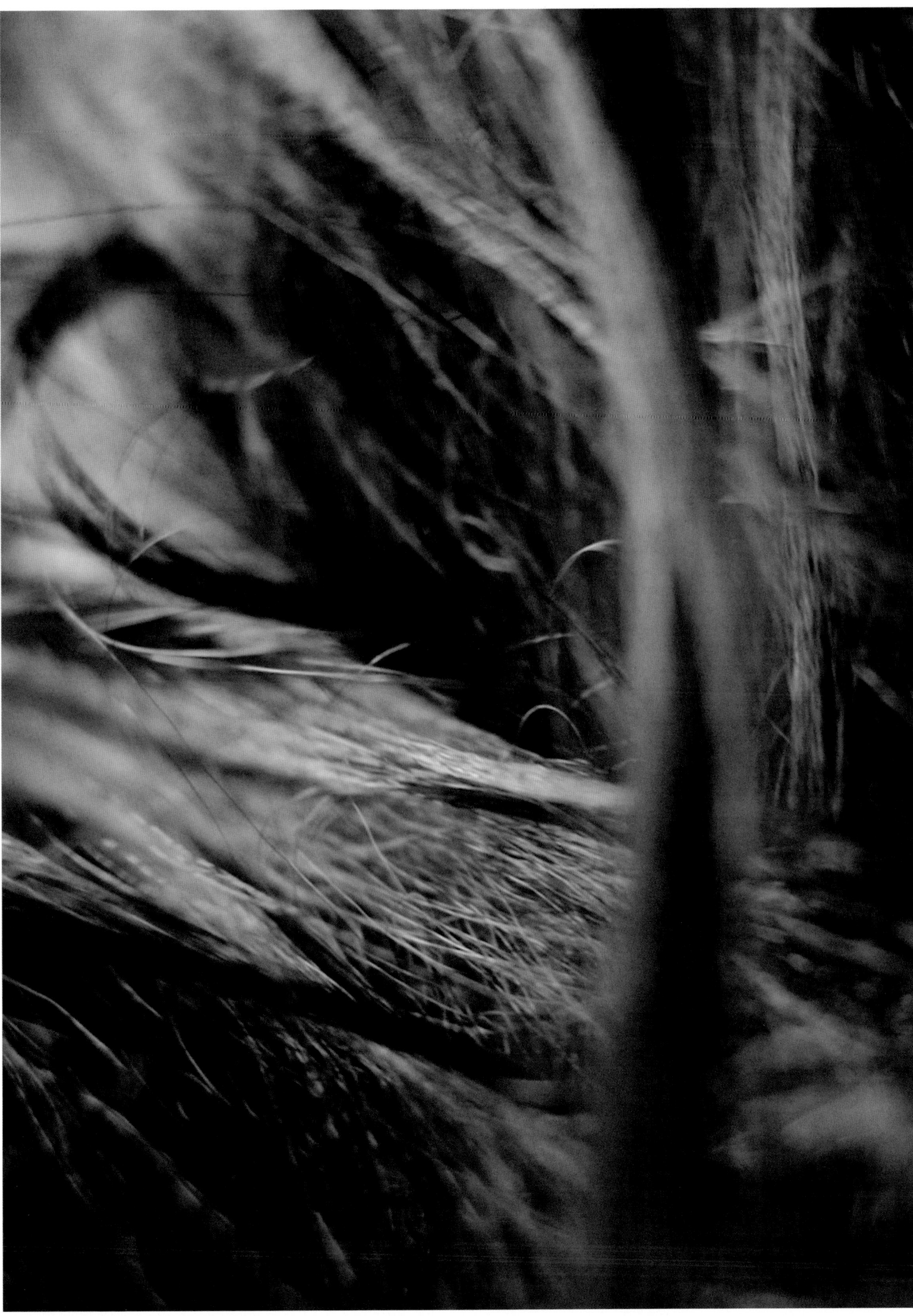

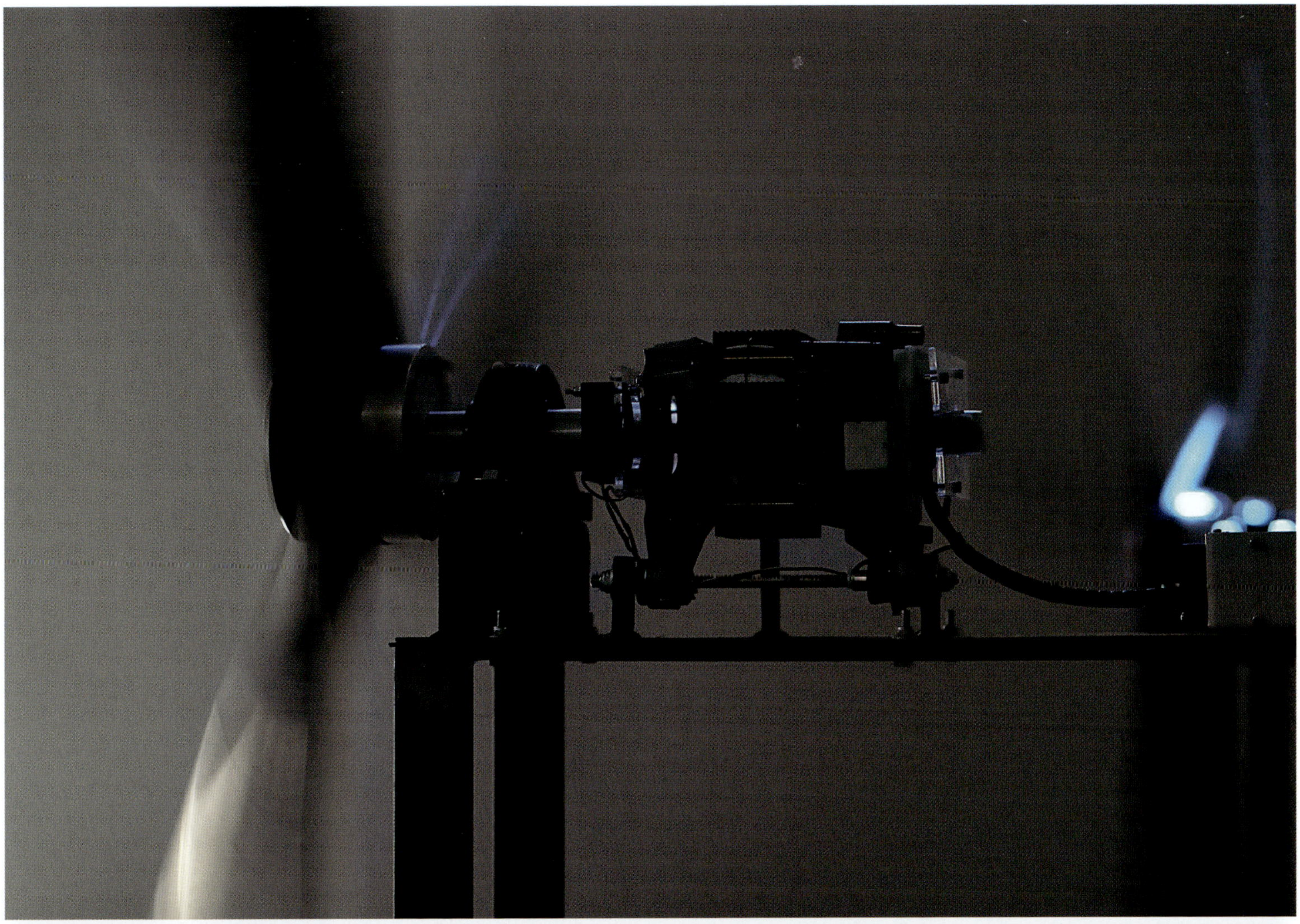

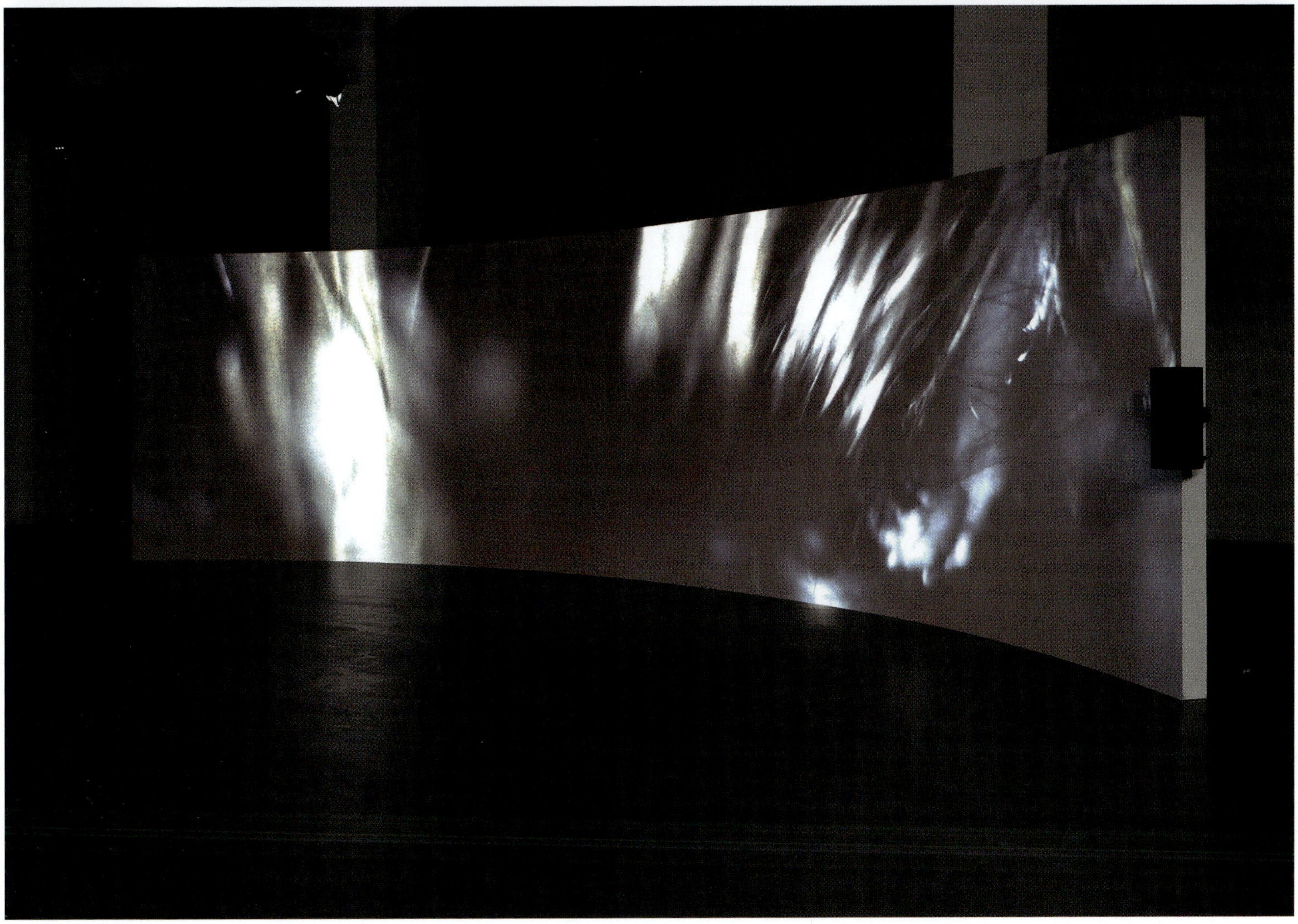

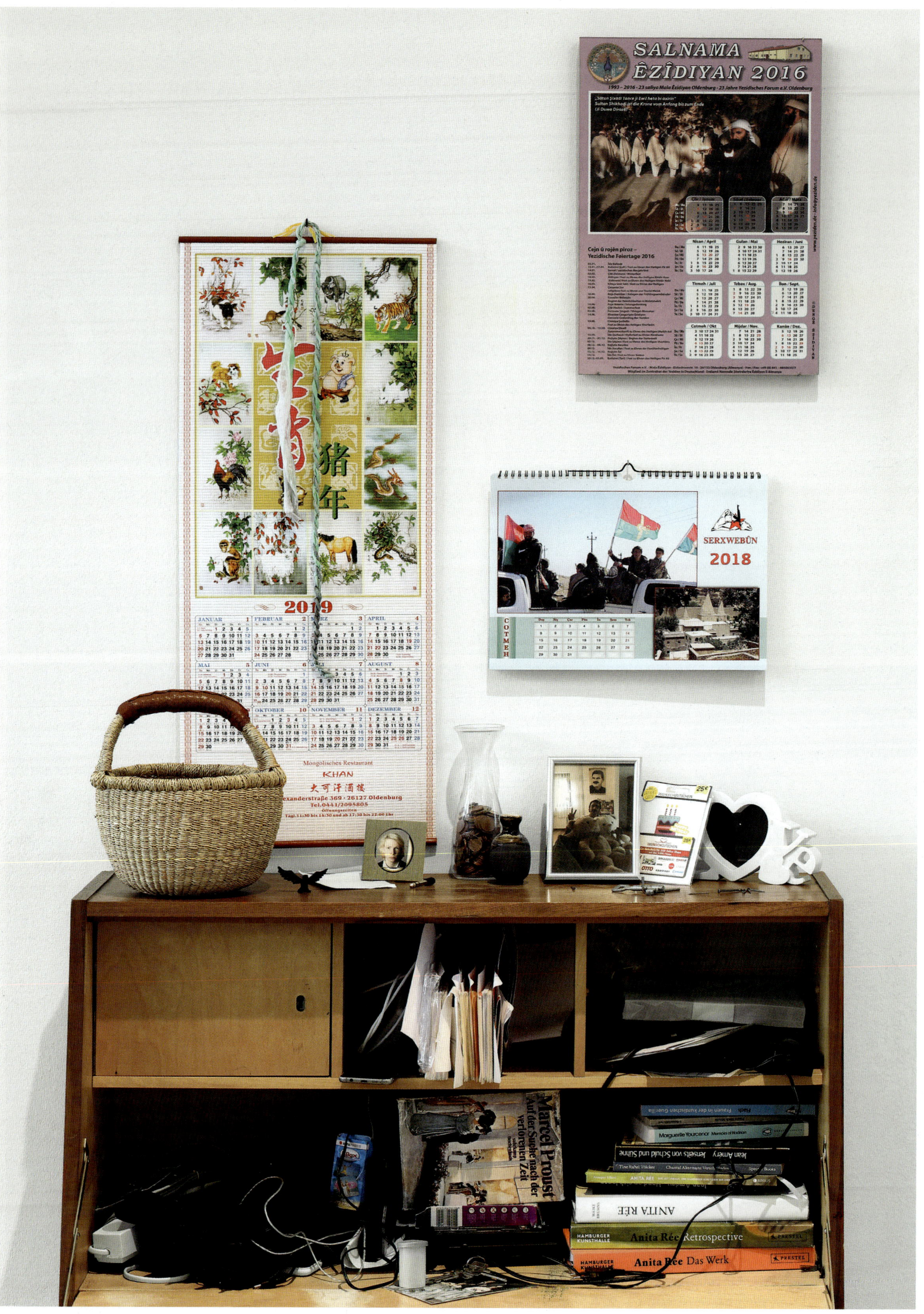

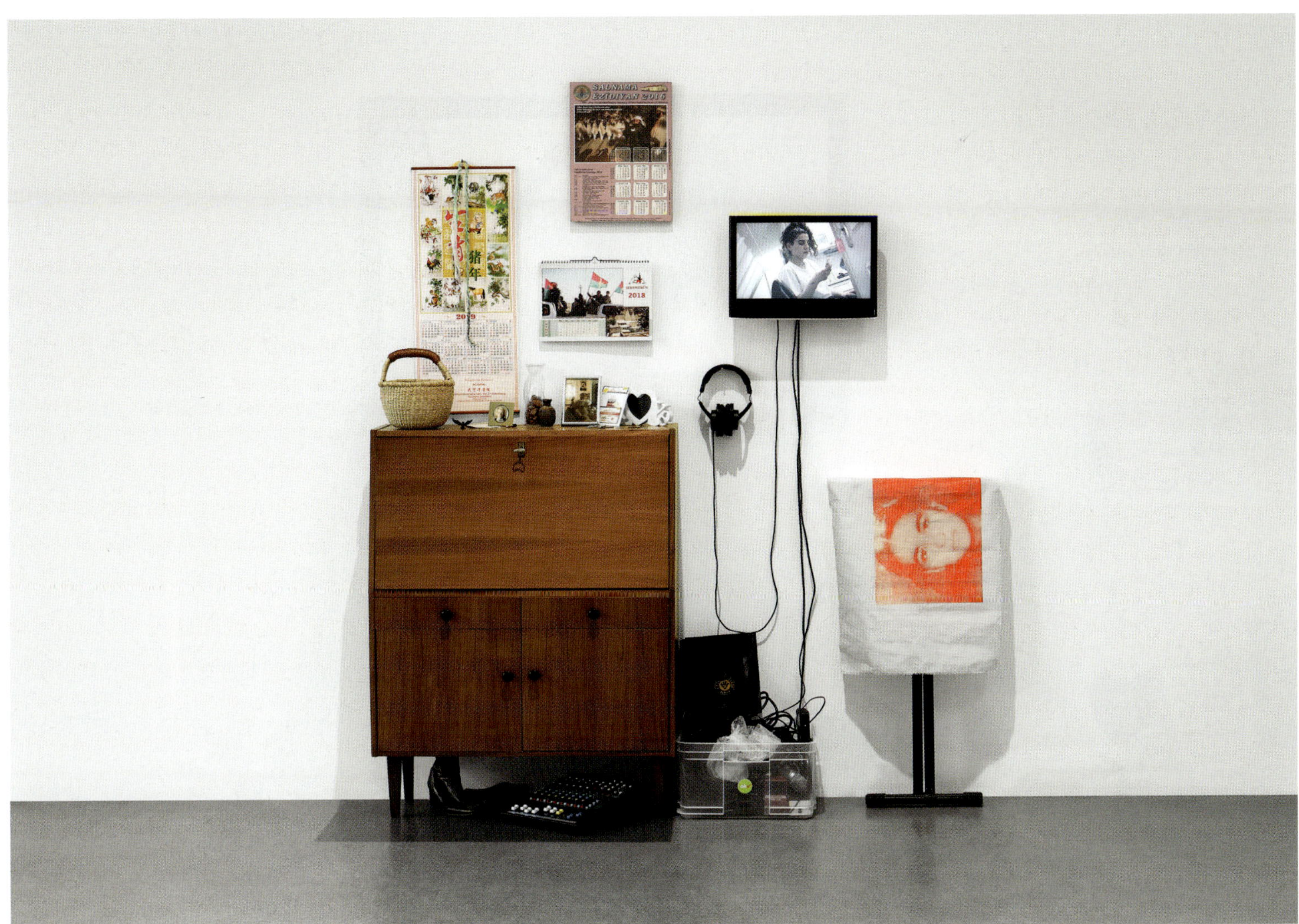

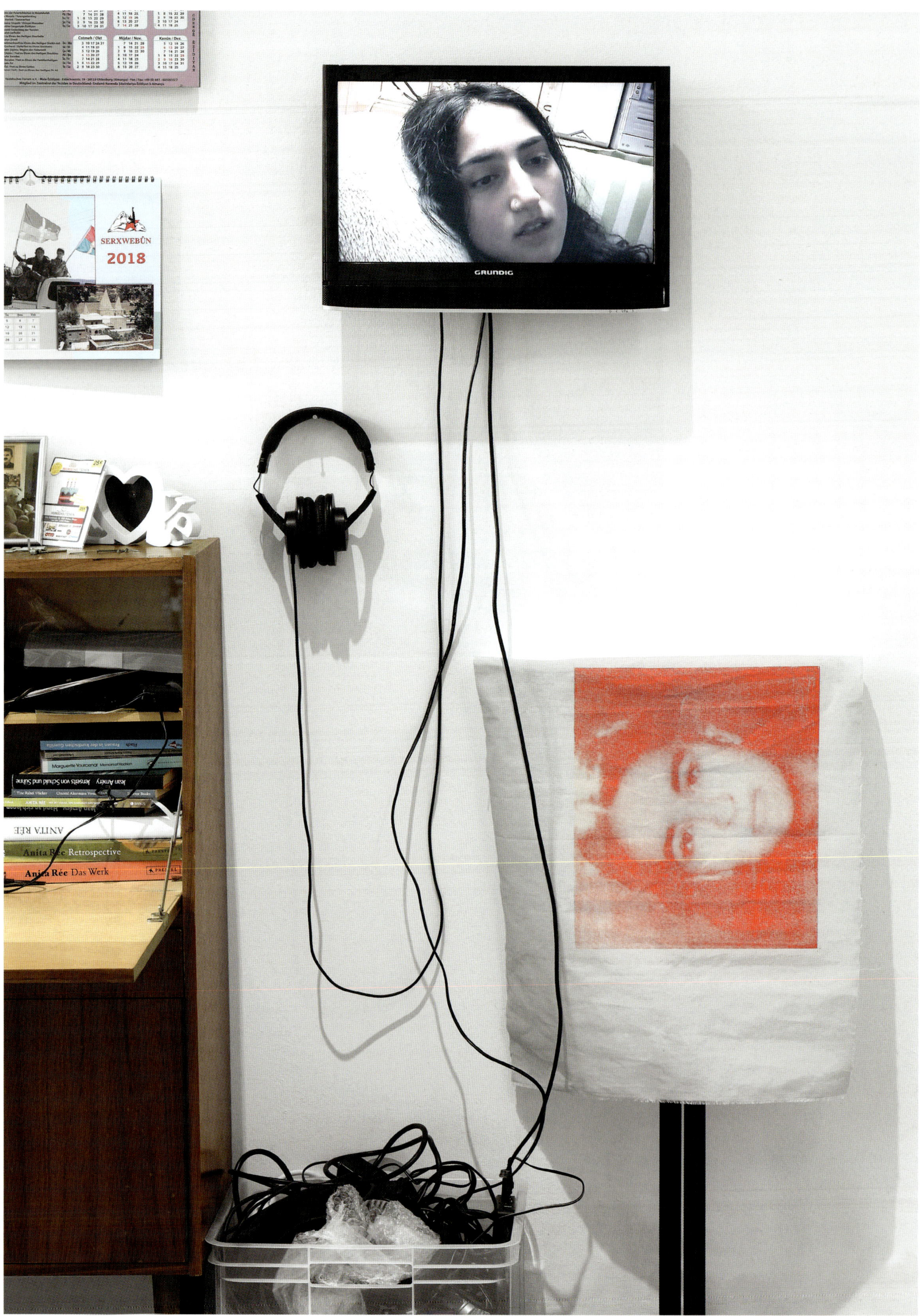

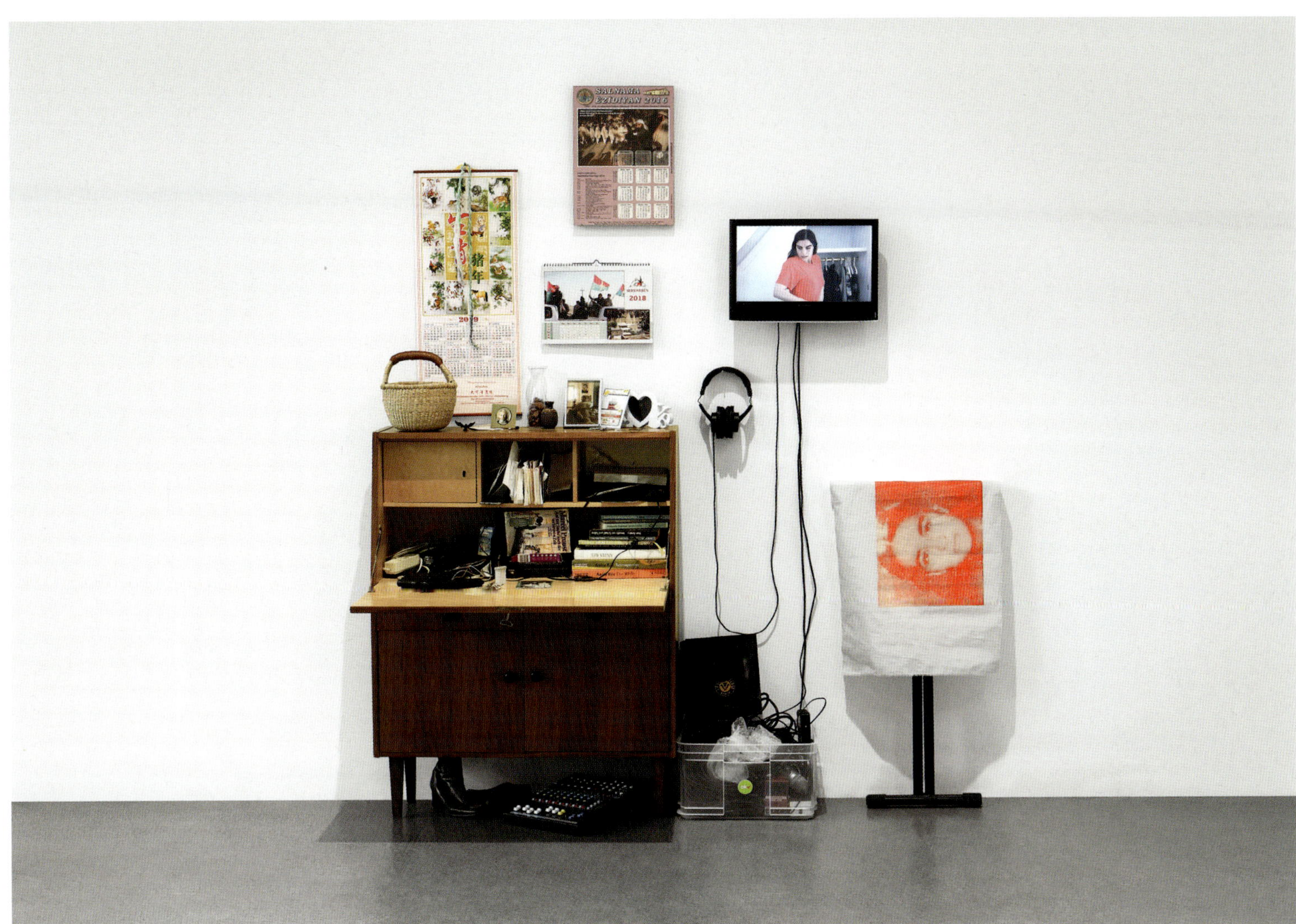

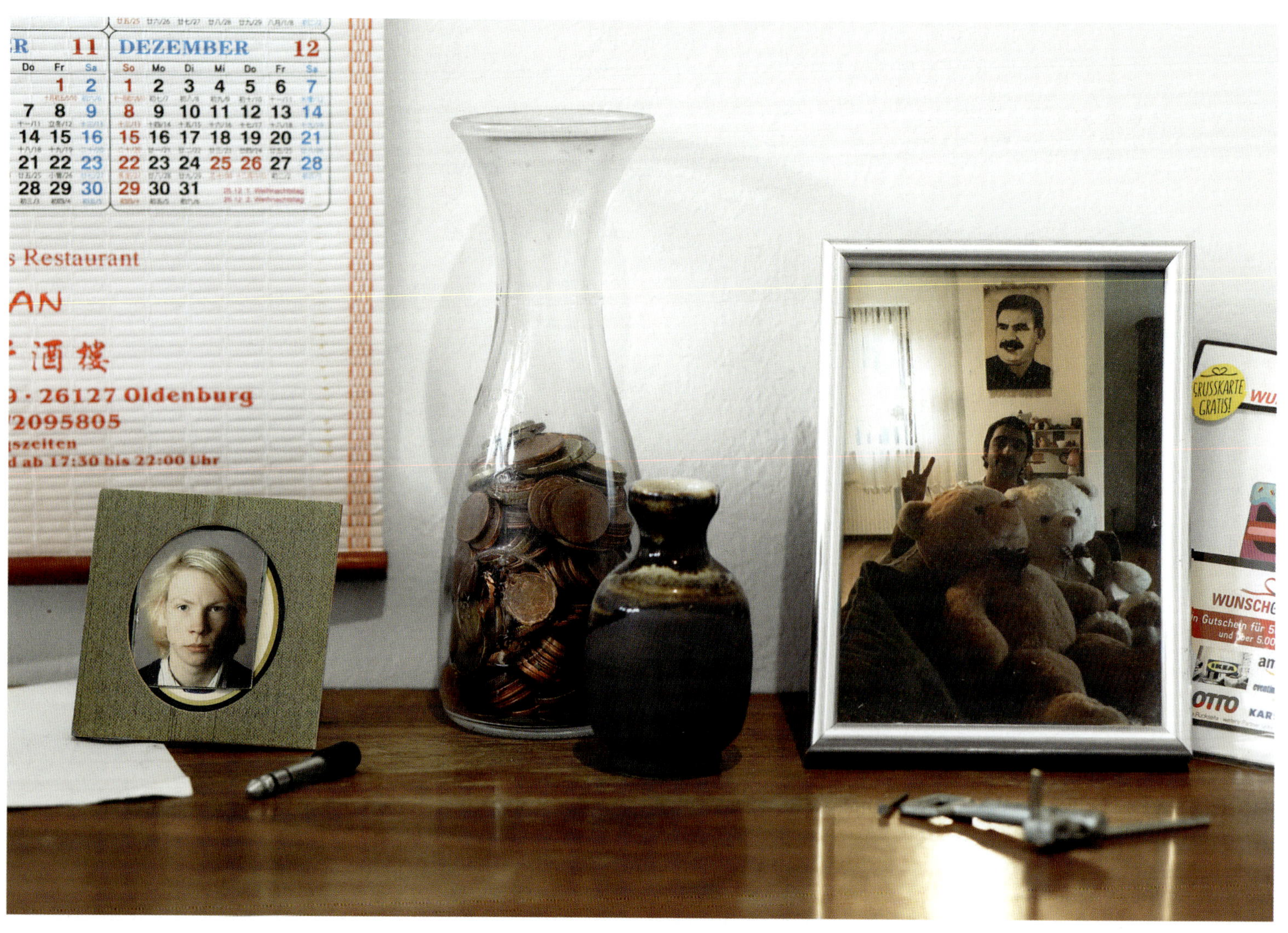
11
DEZEMBER 12
Do Fr Sa
1 2
7 8 9
14 15 16
21 22 23
28 29 30
So Mo Di Mi Do Fr Sa
1 2 3 4 5 6 7
8 9 10 11 12 13 14
15 16 17 18 19 20 21
22 23 24 25 26 27 28
29 30 31
s Restaurant
AN
酒楼
9 · 26127 Oldenburg
2095805
szeiten
d ab 17:30 bis 22:00 Uhr
GRUSSKARTE GRATIS! WU
WUNSCHG
Gutschein für 5
und per 5.00
an
OTTO KAR

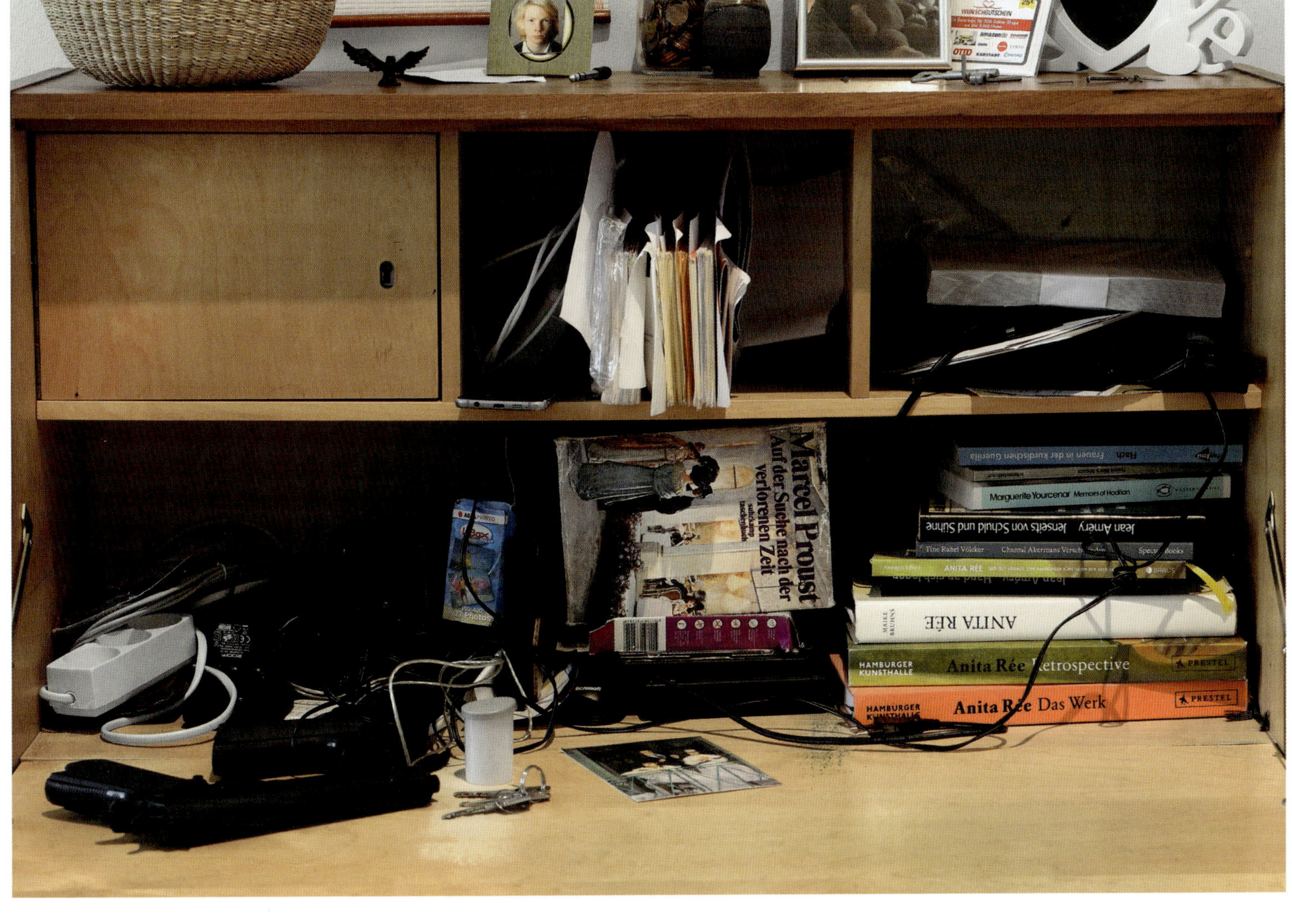

VICTIMS AS POWERFUL ACTORS
Anna Nowak

*What sense does it make [. . .] to continue vegetating in solitude in such
an indescribable world doomed to madness, and to gradually perish inside
from its cruelties?*   Anita Rée, 1933

The Hamburg painter Anita Rée had made her mark. In an art world dominated by men, she took lessons in painting, later encouraged by Max Liebermann. In 1912, Rée, a feminist with Jewish roots, traveled to Paris, where she practiced nude drawing in the circle of Fernand Léger, and absorbed cubist styles and influences from Picasso, Matisse and Cézanne. In 1919, together with other innovative artists, architects and writers, she founded the Hamburg Secession and participated successfully in the association's annual exhibitions. And yet, despite national acclaim, she committed suicide in 1933 on the idyllic vacation island of Sylt. Which circumstances led her to do so?

In 2020, Leyla Yenirce began conducting research on Anita Rée. She collected archival material, journeyed to Sylt in a team together with a performer to probe the artist's doubtful state of mind and to reenact her final days. In the end, a video took shape that establishes the presence of Rée (and of Sylt) through her absence. Long, shimmering, open, black hair can be seen— windblown, universal.

The close-up transforms the sea of hair into a windswept landscape, a typical characteristic of the Frisian island, which is known for its strong gales and white-sanded beaches. The force of nature becomes a projection screen of internal states. The back and forth movement of the waves of hair echo Rée's turmoil, an inner conflict between desires and reality, power and powerlessness. With the rise of National Socialism in the early 1930s, the artist's anxieties and fears of poverty, old age, and isolation increased. She chose the path of emotional release.

Since antiquity, hair has held cultural and social connotations. In manifold representations, hair addressed gender themes, power structures, or cult practices. When hair was cut off, for instance, it testified to humiliation or a new beginning. If hair was piled up high, or particularly long, it represented the forbears, dominance, strength, and the art of seduction. A well-known figure is Loreley who, sitting on a cliff above the Rhine River, drove countless fishermen to their deaths by combing her hair. Already in the classical era, hair also symbolized the human life force and the seat of the soul: a reference that is reflected in the title of the video installation. It is inspired by Walt Whitman's poem *A Clear Midnight* (1881). The American poet addressed it to the soul:

*This is thy hour O Soul, thy free flight into the wordless,
Away from books, away from art, the day erased, the lesson done,
Thee fully forth emerging, silent, gazing, pondering the themes thou lovest best,
Night, sleep, death and the stars.*

It is a kind of mantra of liberating the inner being and creating the space for transcendent themes beyond the constraints of boundaries, place and origin.

FROM VIDEO TO SOUND

In its immediacy, the video installation's compelling audio triggers inner emotions and inscribes itself into the moving images with a new contextualization. Composed of tank noises, digital effects, synthesizers and found footage sounds, it blends with the voices of two resistance activists.

I came to Rojava a year ago as an internationalist. [. . .] Internationalism is a kind of a political thought, that means that everybody who is involved in libationary struggles, it is their duty to not just work for the liberation of their own people or their own area but for everybody.

In 2017, the British activist Anna Campbell travelled to Kurdish-majority, autonomous North and East Syria, also known as Rojava. This region stands for democracy, constitutional law, and the equality of all people, regardless of their ethnicity, religion, or gender. There, she received military training and joined the Kurdish Women's Defense Units (YPJ) to fight against the Turkish forces, which committed severe human rights violations and perpetrated ethnic cleansing. In 2018, she went to the battle front for the first time as Hêlîn Qereçox in Afrin and was killed by a missile attack of the Turkish forces, becoming immortal through the media as a martyr.

Life appears in its temporality. But that which is dead lives and breathes in its descendants. Traumas are often passed on across generations. While Anita Rée took her own life and Anna Campbell risked her life, Lamiya Aji Bashar is fighting to survive.

In 2014, Kocho, Lamiya Aji Bashar's birthplace in Northern Iraq, was heavily attacked by the Islamic State terror militia. As one of many girls and women, she was abducted, abused, enslaved and sold multiple times. In 2016, she and two other young women managed to flee with the aid of local smugglers. One of the women stepped onto a landmine, which nearly caused Aji Bashar to lose her eyesight. Her two companions were killed. She was able to escape and to reach Germany, where since then she has been engaged as a human rights activist for thousands of Yazidi women, who are still in the clutches of ISIS. Here as well we find ethnic cleansing: terror, violent expulsion, deportation and genocide are unleashed by imperialist power politics. In the sound composition of the video, Aji Bashar recounts what happened to her with great courage in Kurdish. Deep anguish is transformed physically and psychologically.

The stories of these women, their struggle for equality, justice and freedom, interweave with each other, accumulating into a united, poignant outcry. "Victims are not only victims, but they are also powerful actors": this catchphrase rings out in a continuous loop.

In September 2022, Mahsa Amini died of a brain hemorrhage, most likely caused by severe violence, under police custody in a Tehran hospital. A few days earlier, she had been arrested by the morality police due to her outward appearance. Her hair was showing from under her hijab. The incident lead to massive, brutal protests in Iran and beyond the national borders. Thousands demonstrated for an investigation of her death; many Iranian female activists tore off their headscarves or burned them in a boycott of the system. They shouted the slogan, "Jin, Jiyan, Azadî"—"Women, Life, and Freedom." Other women

filmed each other while cutting off their hair in solidarity in a gesture of mourning and resistance. The videos spread like wildfire on the web. In the context of a rebellion against patriarchal structures and the oppression of women, the long, black, open, windblown hair of the large-scale projection *Night. Sleep. The Stars.* (2021) becomes an emancipatory symbol of liberation.
The shattered and desecrated body, the surviving body—the technologized body of the future.
A landscape of droning propellers completes the installation. Lined up like soldiers, they emit an enormous, palpable energy, aggressive and threatening. Wind turbines have developed into one of the most potent sources of renewable energy. The Sandbank offshore wind farm 90 kilometers west of the island of Sylt provided the first electricity generated by wind energy from the North Sea to the German power grid. The rotor blades of 23 other wind farms are becoming a defining part of the country's largest nature reserve. Efficiently expanding, they are designed to minimize the effects of global warming. But there is also a downside to this venture. Environmentalists warn against the extinction of biodiversity and pollution through the shipping traffic. Technology as both progress and threat.
Thus, rotors are also used in weapon technology. In 2022, there were over 80 systematic drone attacks in northeast Syria with the aim of weakening democratic self-government in the region. Turkish combat drones are export hits. They are delivered to democracies and dictatorships alike, and have repeatedly bombed Kurdish areas even outside of Turkey, such as the Asos Mountains, in violation of international law. The small, flexible drones are also used for surveillance. The required target acquisition system is the product of a German corporation. The mountains, which once provided protection for the Kurds, are becoming increasingly dangerous. The former idyllic landscape disintegrates into countless pixels (cf. catalogue cover).

FROM SOUND TO PAINTING

Through the written word, technical innovations have emerged; it allows us to communicate across space and time. From common roots, different sign systems were developed, thus also cuneiform writing conceived by the Sumerians around 3,000 BC in what is now Iran and Iraq. Pictograms were the first basic building blocks for writing systems. However, the decisive breakthrough was sound, when images became the first phonetic signs.
Sound is also present in Leyla Yenirce's paintings, not only through the cuneiform script, which in the works recalls a bygone era and simultaneously brings to mind computer codes. Other recurring motifs depict freedom fighters with heavy machine guns, among others from the armed militia YPJ in northern Syria. These are young, idealistic female warriors who are fighting for their Kurdish homeland and, above all, for the liberation of women. The motifs are applied in silkscreen, and are partially barely discernible, partially clearly recognizable. They alternate layer for layer with painted areas. In the manner of a DJ, the selection overlaps, as it is added, from image to image. Thus, historical events and biographies reflecting resilience, violence and resistance are superimposed upon one another. The vigorous, abstract painting gestures on the large-format canvasses are reminiscent of graffiti. As part of hip-hop culture, the rendition of one's individual writing style is a nonviolent competition, in which conflicts are resolved on an artistic level. While graffiti is also referred to as rap writing, Yenirce's working method represents the formulation of noise writing. As a rebellious, radical gesture, the repeated processes of layering on the oversized formats once again involve a lot of energy: this time, it is her own.

VICTIMS
AS POWERFUL ACTORS
Anna Nowak

*Welchen Sinn hat es, (...) in so einer unbeschreiblichen,
dem Wahnsinn verfallenen Welt weiter einsam zu
vegetieren und allmählich an ihren Grausamkeiten
innerlich zugrunde zu gehen?*
Anita Rée, 1933

Die Hamburger Malerin Anita Rée hatte sich durchgesetzt.
In einer von Männern dominierten Kunstwelt nimmt sie
Unterricht in Malerei, wird später von Max Liebermann
zur Kunst ermutigt. 1912 reist die Feministin mit jüdischen
Wurzeln nach Paris, übt sich im Aktzeichnen im Umkreis
von Fernand Léger, greift kubistische Strömungen und
Einflüsse von Picasso, Matisse und Cézanne auf. 1919
gründet sie zusammen mit anderen innovativen KünstlerInnen, ArchitektInnen und LiteratInnen die Hamburgische Sezession und beteiligt sich jährlich erfolgreich an
den Ausstellungen. Doch trotz nationaler Anerkennung
nimmt sie sich 1933 auf der idyllischen Ferieninsel Sylt
das Leben. Welche Umstände haben sie dazu bewegt?

2020 recherchiert Leyla Yenirce zu Anita Rée,
sammelt Archivmaterial, reist im Team mit
einer Darstellerin nach Sylt, um der Verfassung
der zweifelnden Künstlerin nachzuspüren, ihre
letzten Tage zu reinszenieren. Am Ende entsteht
ein Video, das die Anwesenheit Rées (und Sylts)
durch ihre Abwesenheit begründet. Zu sehen ist
langes, schimmerndes, offenes, schwarzes Haar
– wehend, universell.

Die Nahaufnahme macht das Meer an Haaren zu einer
durch Böen bewegten Landschaft – typische Merkmale
der friesischen Insel, bekannt für starken Wind und
weiße Strände. Die Naturgewalt wird zur Projektionsflä-
che innerer Zustände, das Hin und Her der Haarwellen
zur Zerrissenheit Rées, ein innerer Konflikt zwischen
Wünschen und Wirklichkeit – Macht und Ohnmacht.
Mit dem Aufstieg der NSDAP Anfang der 1930er Jahre
nahmen die Sorgen und Ängste der Künstlerin vor
Verarmung, Alter und Isolation zu. Sie entscheidet sich
für seelische Erlösung.

Seit der Antike haben Haare kultur- und sozi-
algesellschaftliche Konnotationen. Sie thema-
tisierten in vielfältigen Darstellungen Gender-
Sujets, Machtstrukturen oder Kult-Handlungen.
War das Haar abgeschnitten, bezeugte es bei-
spielsweise Demütigung oder Neubeginn.
Wurde es hochgesteckt oder war besonders
lang, stand es für die AhnInnen, Dominanz,
Stärke und Verführungskunst. Bekannt ist die
auf dem Rheinfelsen thronende Loreley, die mit
dem Kämmen ihrer Haare unzählige Fischer in
den Tod lotste. Bereits im klassischen Altertum
symbolisierte Haar auch die Lebenskraft des
Menschen und den Sitz der Seele. Ein Bezug,
der sich im Titel der Videoinstallation wieder-
findet. Dieser lehnt sich an das 1881 verfasste
Gedicht *Eine lichte Mitternacht* von Walt Whitman an. Der US-amerikanische Lyriker adres-
siert es an die Seele:

*Dies ist deine Stunde, o Seele, dein freier Flug ins Wortlose,
Fort von Büchern, weg von Künsten, nach getilgtem Tag, nach
getaner Arbeit,
Dich ganz und weit forthebend, schwelgend, staunend, sinnend über
das, was du am meisten liebtest: Nacht, Schlaf, Tod und die Sterne.*

Es ist eine Art Mantra, das Innere zu befreien
und den Raum für transzendente Themen zu
schaffen, grenzen-, orts- und herkunftslos.

AUS DEM VIDEO ZUM SOUND
Der eindringliche Sound der multimedialen Installation löst in seiner Unmittelbarkeit innere Ergriffenheit aus und schreibt sich in das Bewegtbild mit einem neuen Kontext ein. Bestehend aus Panzergeräuschen, digitalen Effekten, Synthesizern und Found Footage-Klängen mischt er sich mit Stimmen zweier Widerstandsaktivistinnen.

Ich kam vor einem Jahr als Internationalistin nach Rojava. (...) Internationalismus ist eine Art politischer Gedanke, der bedeutet, dass jeder, der sich an Befreiungskämpfen beteiligt, die Pflicht hat, nicht nur für die Befreiung seines eigenen Volkes oder seiner eigenen Region zu handeln, sondern für alle.

2017 reist die britische Aktivistin Anna Campbell in das kurdisch geprägte, autonome Nord- und Ostsyrien, auch bekannt unter dem Namen Rojava. Die Gebiete stehen für Demokratie, Rechtsstaatlichkeit und Gleichberechtigung aller Menschen, unabhängig von Ethnie, Religion oder Geschlecht. Dort erhält sie eine militärische Ausbildung und schließt sich den kurdischen Frauenverteidigungseinheiten (YPJ) an, um gegen die türkische Besatzung zu kämpfen, die schwerwiegende Menschenrechtsverletzungen begehen und ethnische Säuberung verüben. 2018 geht sie als Hêlîn Qereçox zum ersten Mal in der Schlacht von Afrin an die Front und wird vom Raketenangriff der türkischen Streitkräfte getötet – medial wird sie als Märtyrerin unsterblich.
Das Leben erscheint in seiner Zeitlichkeit. Doch auch was tot ist, lebt und atmet im Nachgeborenen. Traumata werden häufig transgenerational übertragen. Während Anita Rée sich das Leben nimmt, Anna Campbell ihr Leben riskiert, kämpft Lamiya Aji Bashar ums Überleben.
2014 ist Kocho, Lamiya Aji Bashars Geburtsort, im Nordirak durch die Terrormiliz Islamischer Staat von Übergriffen stark betroffen. Als eine von vielen Mädchen und Frauen wird sie entführt, missbraucht, versklavt und mehrmals verkauft. 2016 entkommt sie mit zwei weiteren jungen Frauen durch lokale SchmugglerInnen. Eine der Frauen tritt auf eine Landmine, wodurch Aji Bashar fast ihr Augenlicht verliert. Die beiden BegleiterInnen werden getötet. Sie entkommt, gelangt nach Deutschland und setzt sich seitdem als Menschenrechtsaktivistin für tausende jesidische Frauen ein, die sich noch immer in der Gewalt des IS befinden. Auch hier ethnische Säuberung: Terror, gewaltsame Vertreibung, Deportation und Genozid ausgelöst durch imperialistische Machtpolitik. Mit ungeheurem Mut erzählt Aji Bashar auf Kurdisch in der Soundkomposition des Videos das, was ihr widerfahren ist. Der tiefe Schmerz transformiert sich physisch und psychisch.
Die Geschichten dieser Frauen, ihr Kampf für Gleichheit, Gerechtigkeit und Freiheit verweben sich miteinander, so dass sich ihr vereinter Aufschrei in einer schrillen Tonfrequenz akkumuliert. „Victims are not only victims, but they are also powerful actors", erklingt als Parole in Dauerschleife.
Im September 2022 stirbt Mahsa Amini in Teheran unter Polizeigewahrsam in einem Krankenhaus an einer Hirnblutung, höchstwahrscheinlich durch schwere Gewalt ausgelöst. Ein paar Tage zuvor war sie von der Sitten- und Religionspolizei wegen ihres äußeren Auftretens verhaftet worden. Ihr Haar lugte unter ihrem Hijab hervor. Der Vorfall führt im Iran und außerhalb der Landesgrenzen zu massiven, brutalen Protesten. Tausende demonstrieren für die Aufklärung des Todesfalls, viele iranische Aktivistinnen reißen sich dabei das Kopftuch herunter oder verbrennen es als Boykottierung des Systems. „Jin – Jiyan – Azadi", rufen sie, „Frauen, Leben, Freiheit". Andere Frauen filmen sich dabei, wie sie

sich aus Solidarität in einer Trauer- und Widerstandsgeste die Haare abschneiden. Die Videos verbreiten sich wie Lauffeuer im Netz. In dem Kontext des Aufbegehrens gegen patriarchale Strukturen und die Unterdrückung der Frau wird langes – schwarzes – offenes – wehendes Haar als großformatige Projektion von *Nacht. Schlaf. Die Sterne.*, 2021 zum emanzipatorischen Symbol der Befreiung.

Der zersprengte und geschändete Körper, der überlebende Körper – der technologisierte Zukunftskörper. Eine Landschaft aus dröhnenden Propellern ergänzt die Installation. Sie lösen eine enorme, spürbare Energie aus, aggressiv und bedrohlich, aufgereiht wie SoldatInnen. Windkraftanlagen haben sich zu einer der stärksten erneuerbaren Energiequellen entwickelt. Der Offshore-Windpark Sandbank 90 Kilometer westlich der Insel Sylt hat den ersten Strom aus Windenergie von der Nordsee in das deutsche Stromnetz eingespeist. Rotorblätter von 23 weiteren Windparks fügen sich in die Region des größten Naturschutzgebietes des Landes ein. Effizient expandieren sollen sie, die Auswirkungen der globalen Erwärmung minimieren. Doch es gibt auch eine Kehrseite dieses Vorhabens. UmweltschützerInnen warnen vor dem Aussterben der Artenvielfalt und Umweltverschmutzung durch Schiffsverkehr. Die Technik als Fortschritt und Bedrohung zugleich.

So kommen Rotoren auch in der Waffentechnologie zum Einsatz. 2022 gab es über achtzig systematische Drohnenangriffe in Nordostsyrien mit dem Ziel die demokratische Selbstverwaltung in der Region zu schwächen. Türkische Kampfdrohnen sind dabei Exportschlager, werden an Demokratien und Diktaturen geliefert und bombardieren völkerrechtswidrig kurdische Gebiete wie die Asos-Berge, sogar außerhalb der Türkei. Die kleinen, flexiblen Luftfahrzeuge dienen auch der Überwachung. Das dafür notwendige Zielerfassungssystem ist ein Produkt eines deutschen Konzerns. Die einst für die KurdInnen schutzbietenden Berge werden zur Gefahr. Die ehemals idyllische Landschaft zerfällt in unzählige Pixel (vgl. Katalogcover).

AUS DEM SOUND ZUR MALEREI

Durch Schrift sind technische Innovationen entstanden, sie ermöglicht uns über Raum und Zeit hinweg zu kommunizieren. Aus gemeinsamen Wurzeln wurden unterschiedliche Zeichensysteme entwickelt, so auch etwa 3.000 v. Chr. von den SumererInnen die Keilschrift in den Gebieten des heutigen Iran und Irak. Piktogramme waren die ersten Grundbausteine für Schriftsysteme, doch der entscheidende Durchbruch war der Klang, als Bilder zu den ersten Lautzeichen wurden.

Sound gibt auch die Malerei von Leyla Yenirce wieder, nicht nur durch die Keilschrift, die in den Arbeiten an eine vergangene Epoche und gleichzeitig an Computercodes erinnert. Weitere wiederkehrende Motive zeigen Freiheitskämpferinnen mit schweren Maschinengewehren, unter anderem von der bewaffneten Miliz YPJ in Nordsyrien. Es sind junge, idealistische Kriegerinnen, die für ihre kurdische Heimat kämpfen und vor allem für die Befreiung der Frau. Die Motive sind in Siebdruck aufgetragen, teilweise nur zu erahnen, teilweise deutlich erkennbar. Sie wechseln sich Schicht für Schicht mit Farbaufträgen ab. Wie bei einem DJ greift die Auswahl beim Auflegen von Bild zu Bild ineinander über. So überlagern sich historische Ereignisse und Biografien, die Resilienz, Gewalt und Widerstand reflektieren. Die schwungvollen, abstrakten Malgesten auf den großformatigen Leinwänden erinnern an Graffiti. Als Teil der Hip-Hop-Kultur ist der Writing-Style ein gewaltfreier Wettstreit, bei dem Konflikte auf künstlerischer Ebene ausgetragen werden. Während Graffiti auch als Rapschrift bezeichnet wird, so steht Yenirces Arbeitsweise für die Formulierung einer Noiseschrift. Eine eher auflehnende, radikale Geste, bei der es durch das wiederholende *Layern* auf den übergroßen Formaten wieder einmal um sehr viel Energie geht – dieses Mal ist es ihre eigene.

CIRCLE
Leyla Yenirce

I am in a circle. I am in my circle. I am there. Around me is a circle. The contours of a circle.
I sit in the center while drawing the edges with a pencil.
It belongs only to me. The circle. It is my circle and the boundaries I draw, I determine.
And things happen around me that do something to me, but they don't enter my circle.
They stop in front of the contours.
In my circle it is quiet, there I am, nothing happens. Nothing happens. Absolutely nothing.
It is silent. There is a body and a soul there and they exist.
The only thing that beats is the heart in this body in this circle, the only thing that thinks, the spirit
in this body in this circle and from there it transforms, shifts outside, from inside to outside,
out of the circle. But the contours are still fresh, I'm not letting anyone in.

KREIS
Leyla Yenirce

Ich bin in einem Kreis. Ich bin in meinem Kreis. Ich bin da. Um mich herum
ist ein Kreis. Die Konturen eines Kreises. Ich sitze in der Mitte, während ich
mit einem Stift die Ränder zeichne.
Er gehört nur mir. Der Kreis. Es ist mein Kreis und die Grenzen ziehe ich,
ich bestimme.
Und um mich herum passieren Dinge, die etwas mit mir machen, aber sie
gelangen nicht in meinen Kreis. Sie bleiben vor den Konturen stehen.
In meinem Kreis ist es leise, dort bin ich da, es passiert nichts. Es passiert
nichts. Absolut nichts. Es ist still. Dort ist ein Körper und eine Seele und
sie existieren.
Das Einzige, was schlägt, ist das Herz in diesem Körper in diesem Kreis,
das Einzige, was denkt, der Geist in diesem Körper in diesem Kreis
und von dort aus wandelt er um, verlagert nach draußen, aus dem Inneren
nach außen, raus aus dem Kreis. Aber die Konturen sind noch frisch,
ich lasse niemanden rein.

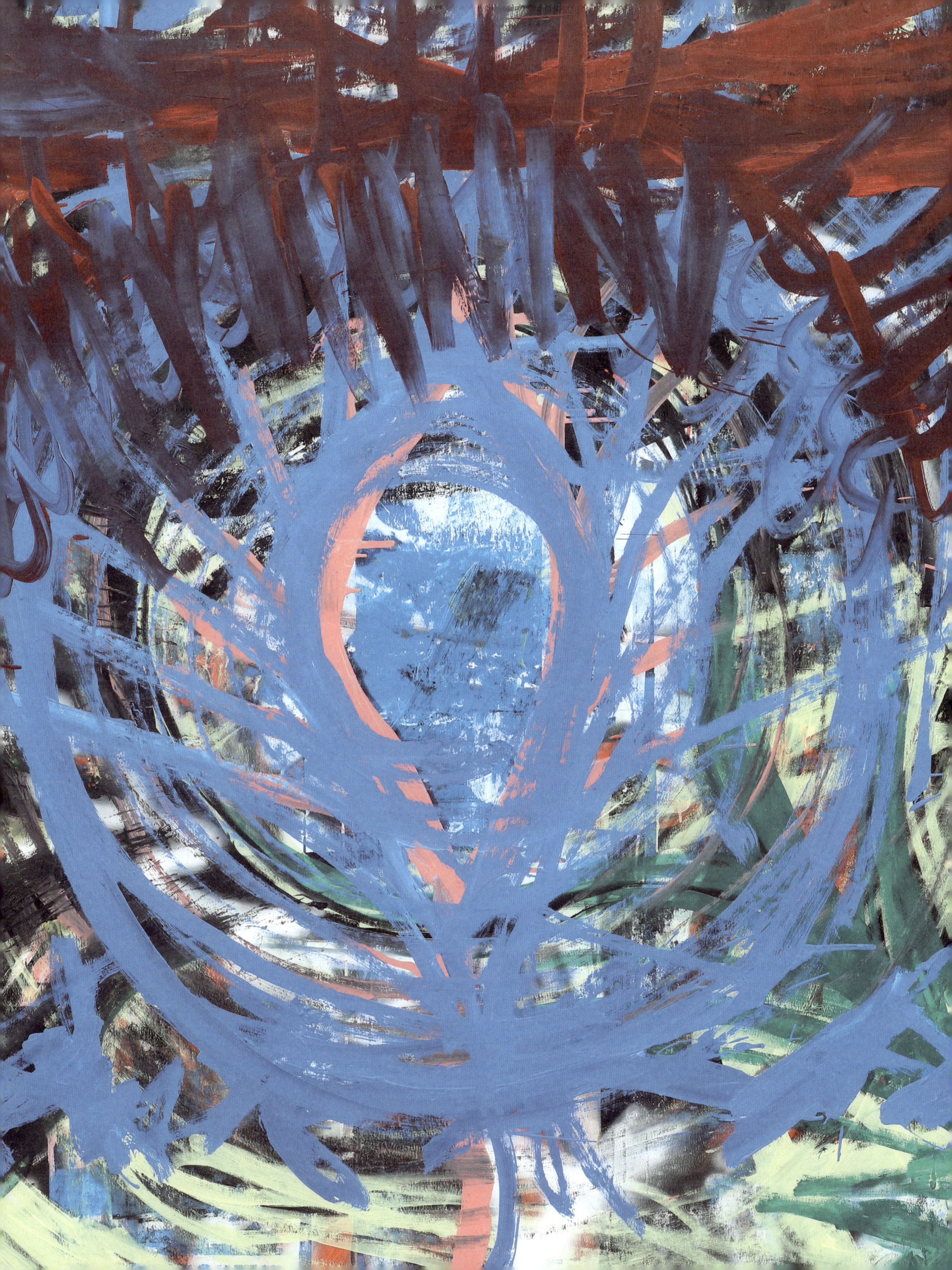

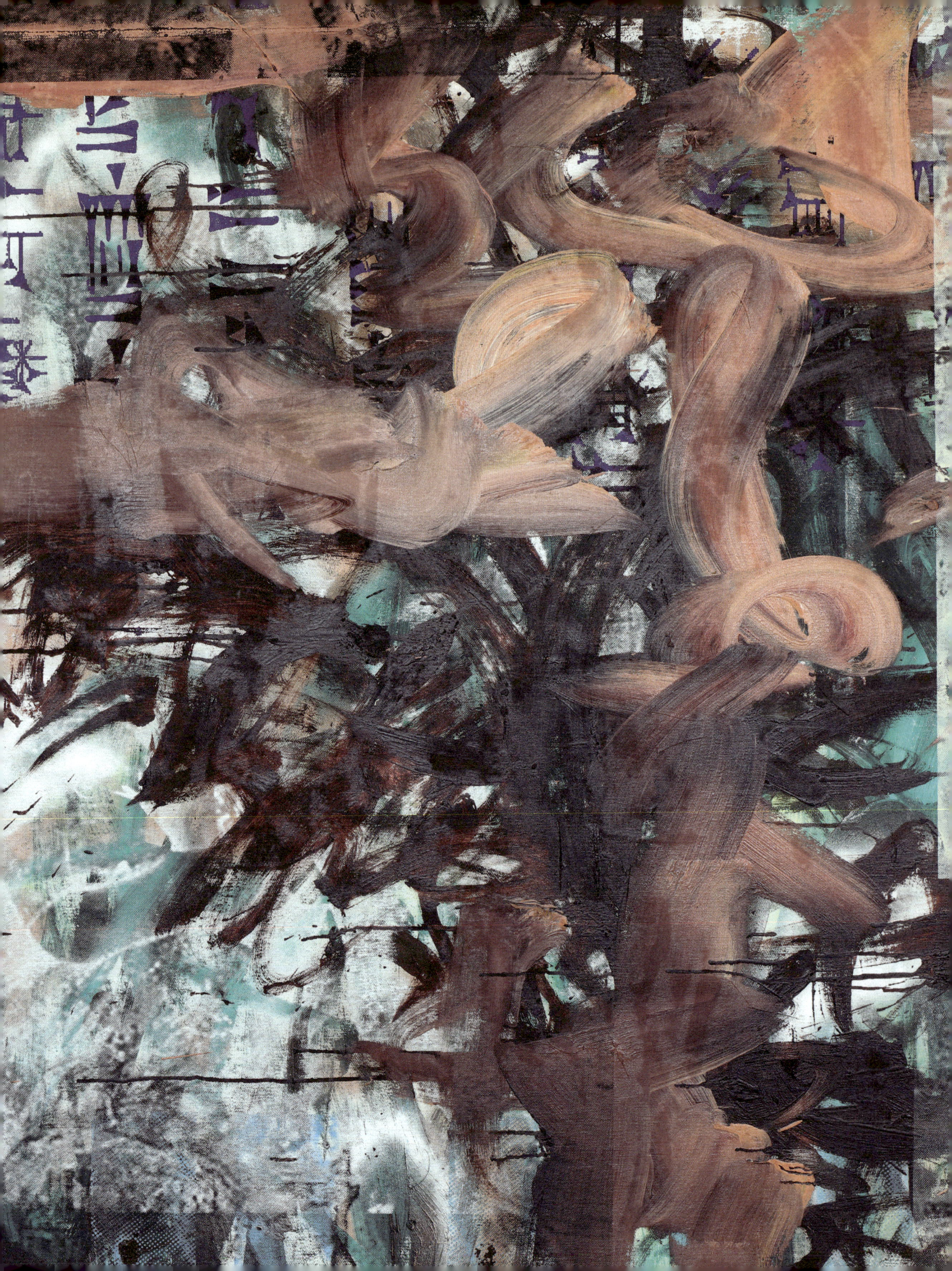

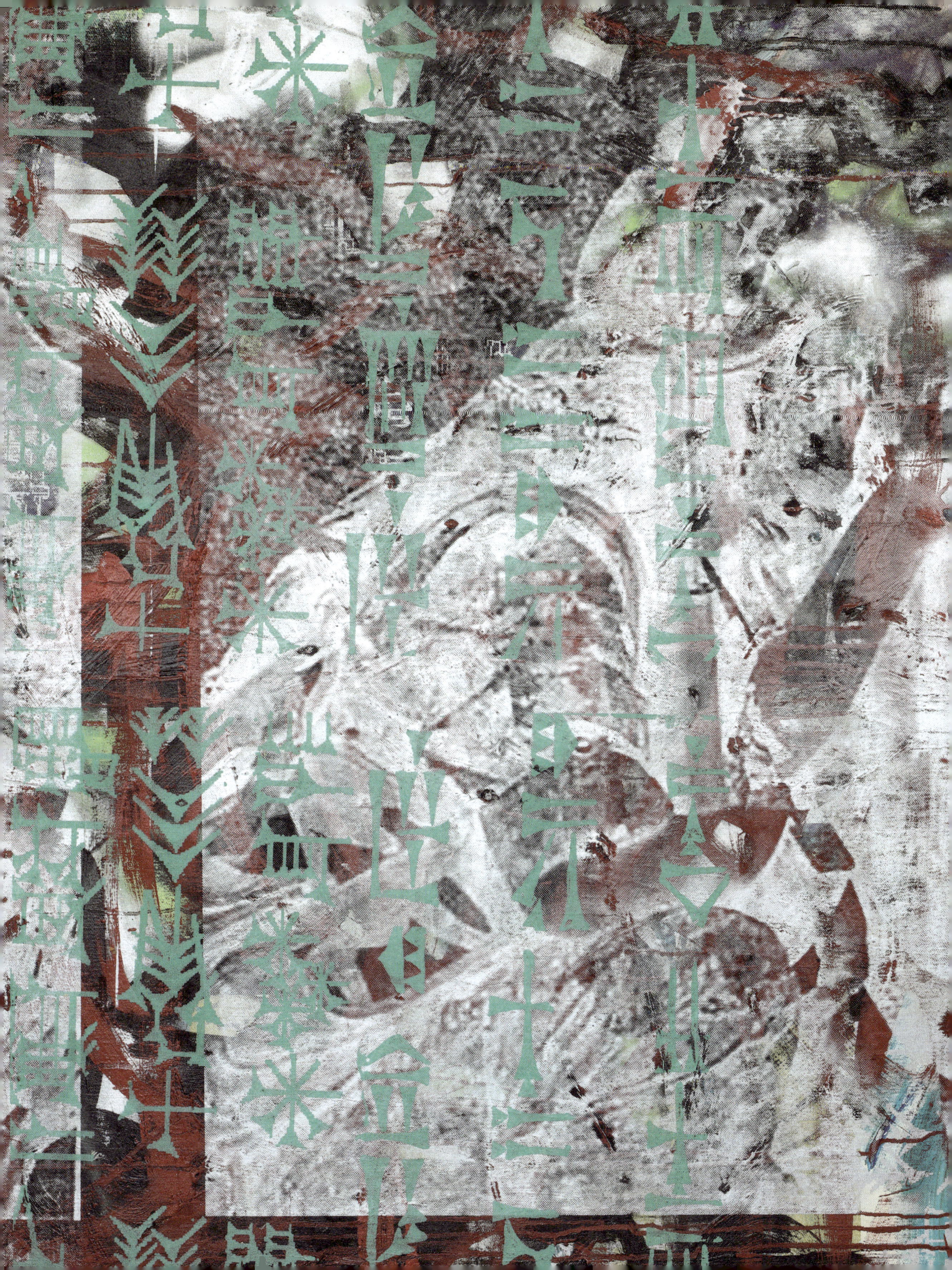

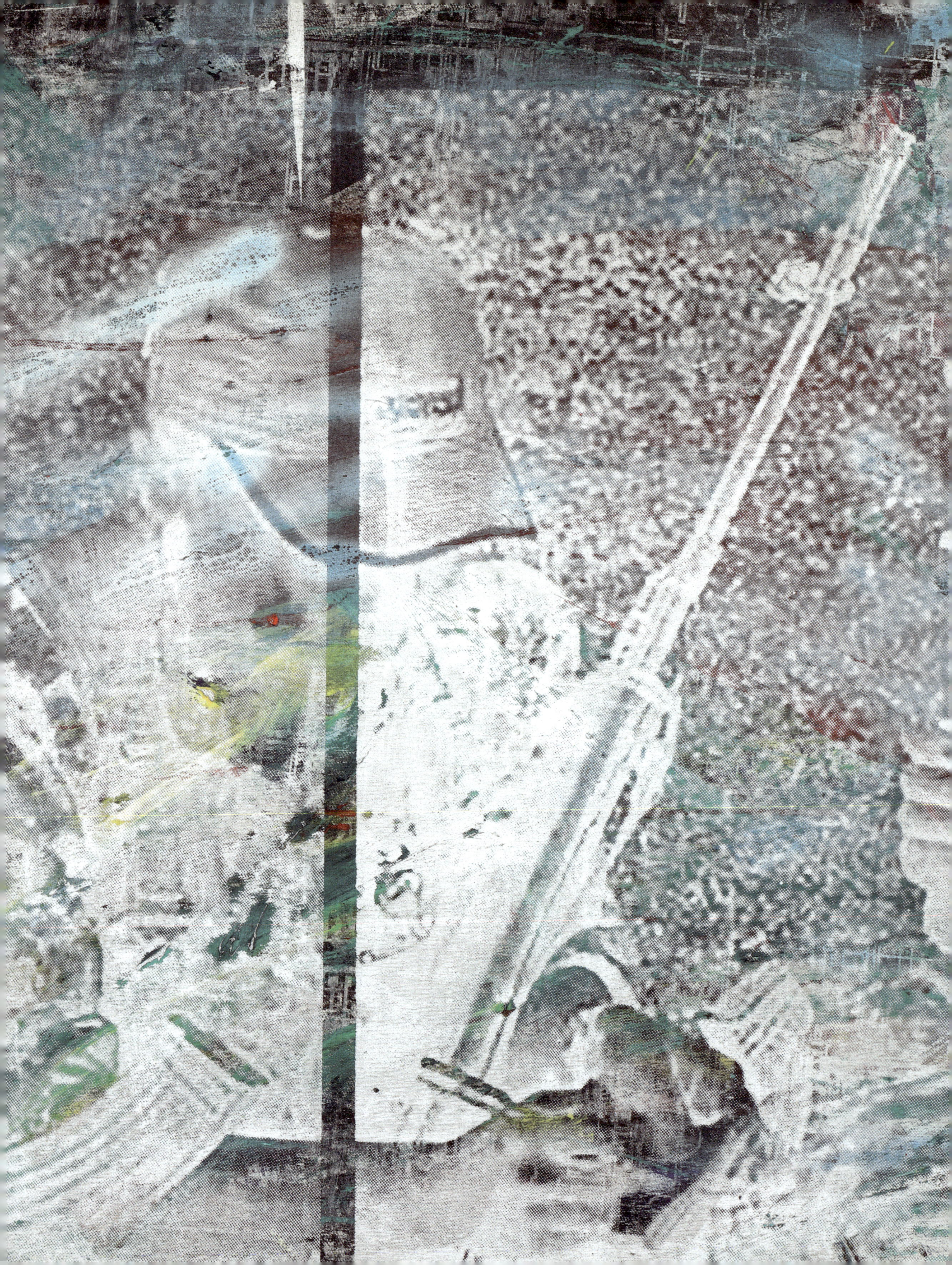

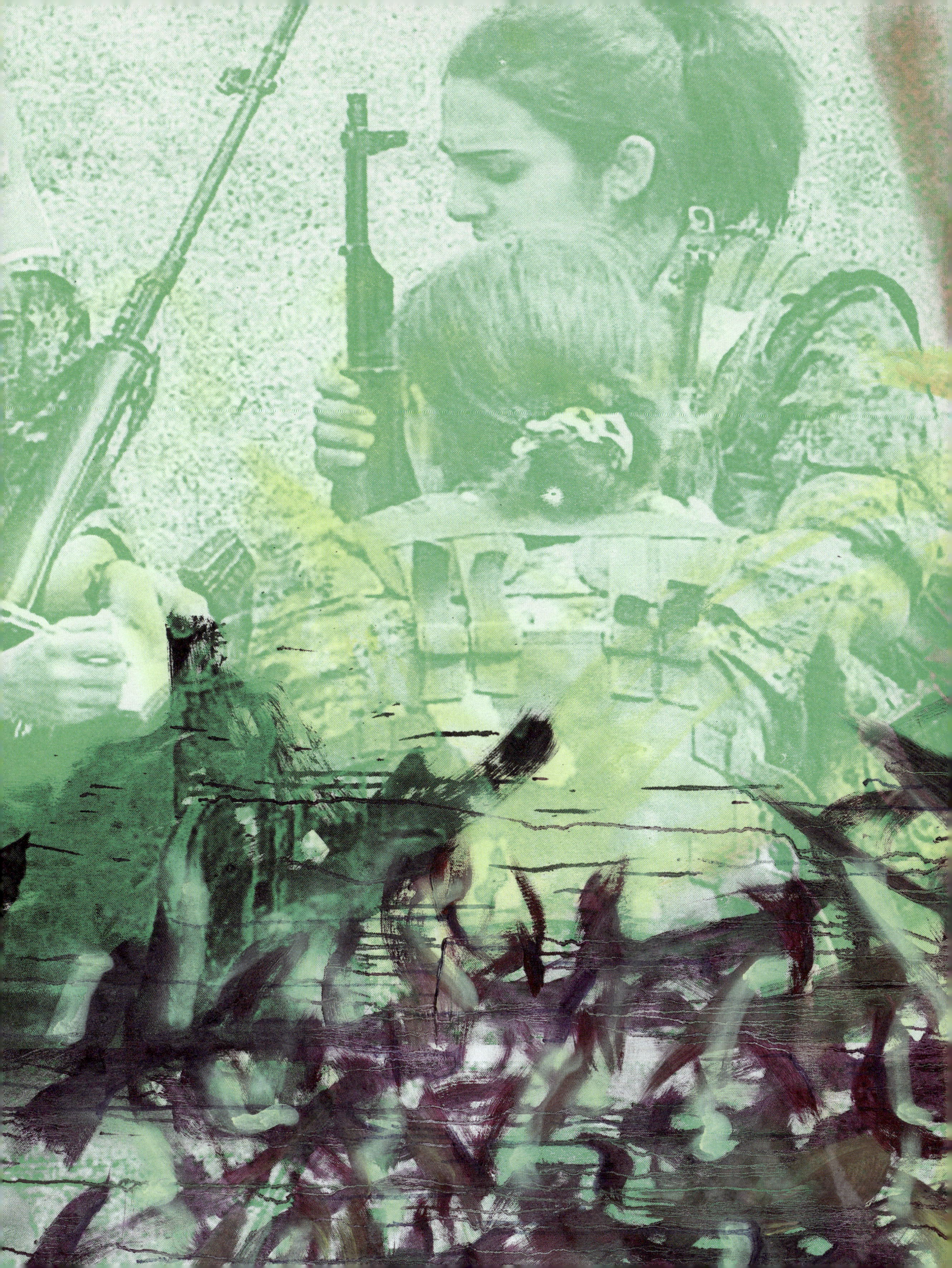

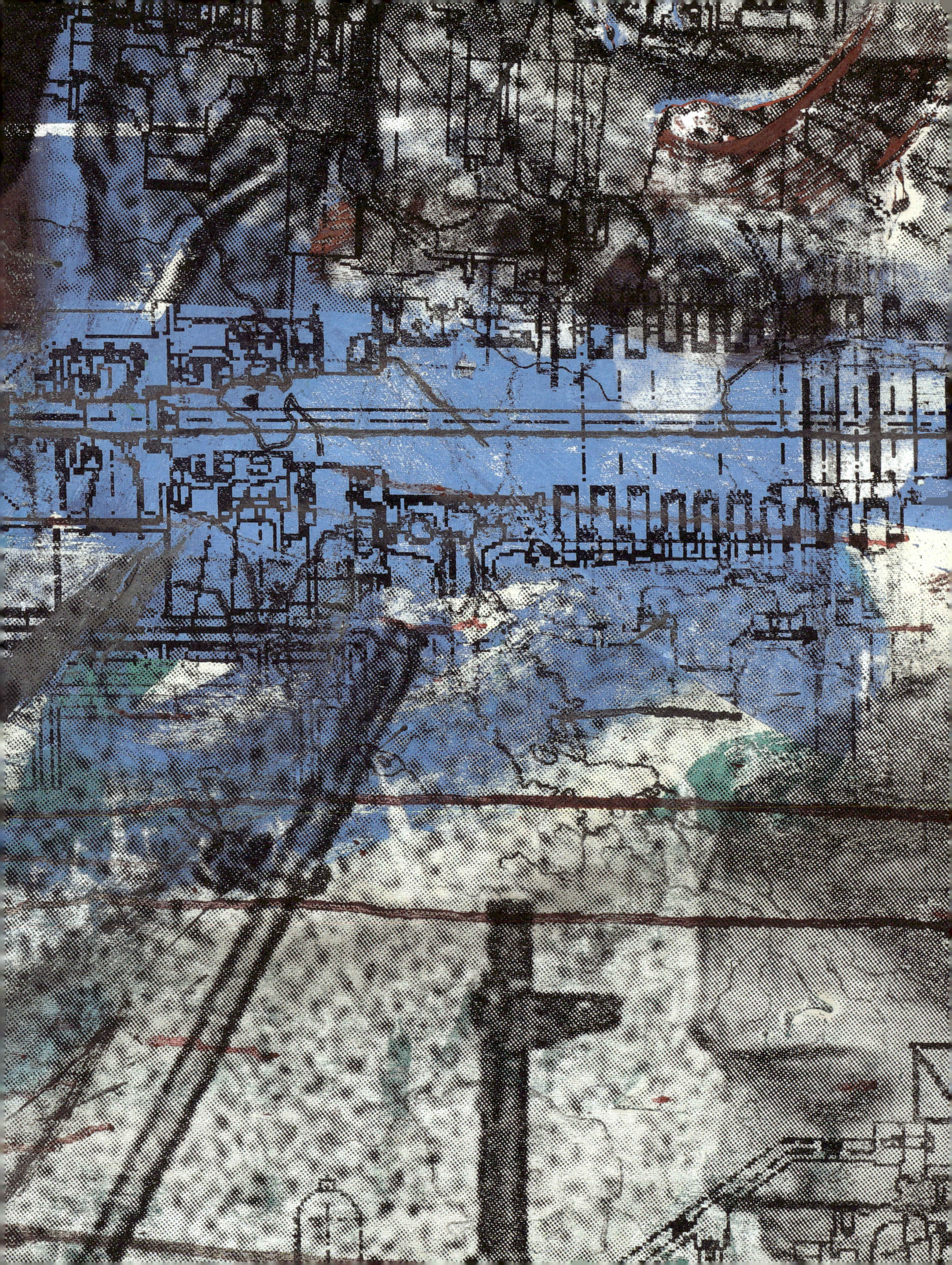

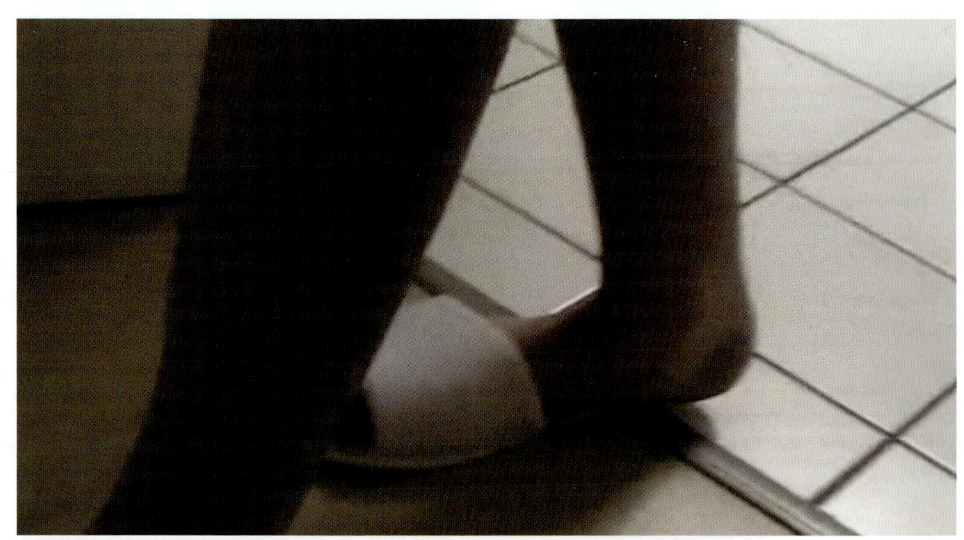
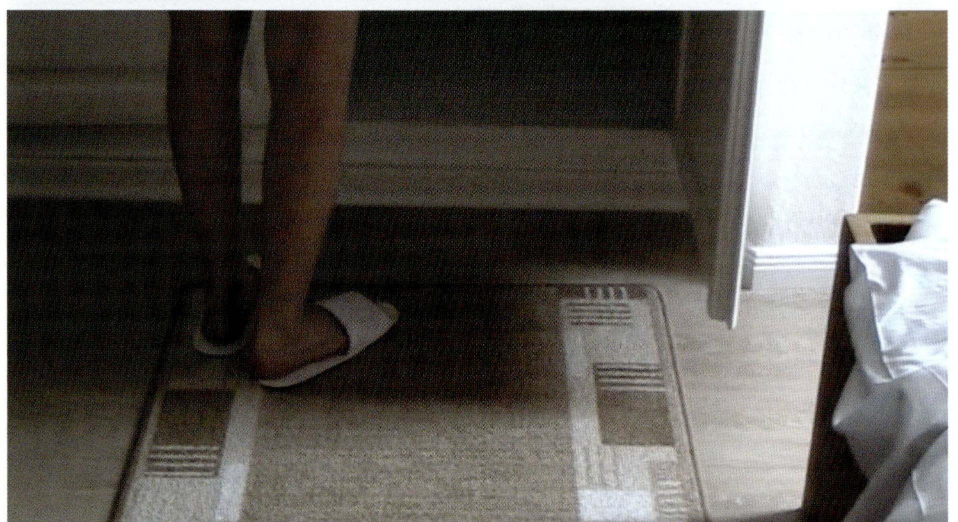
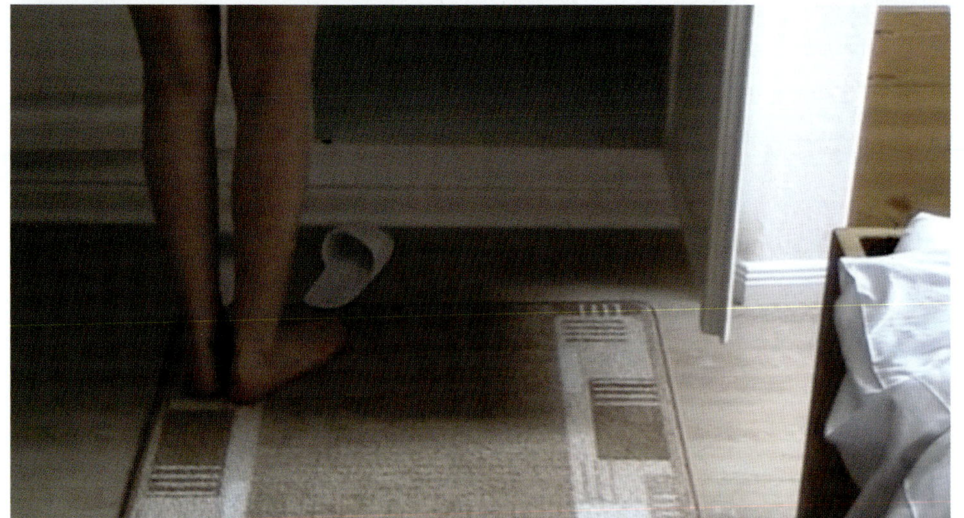
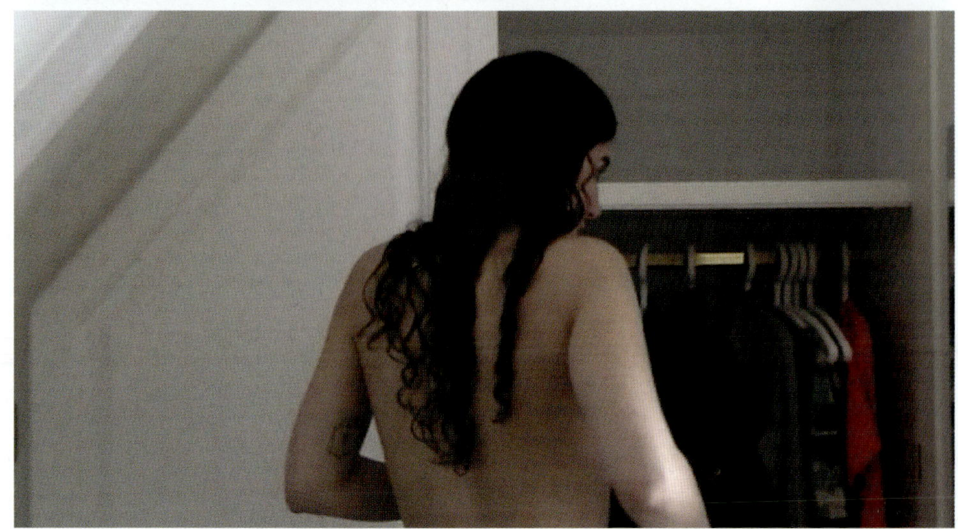

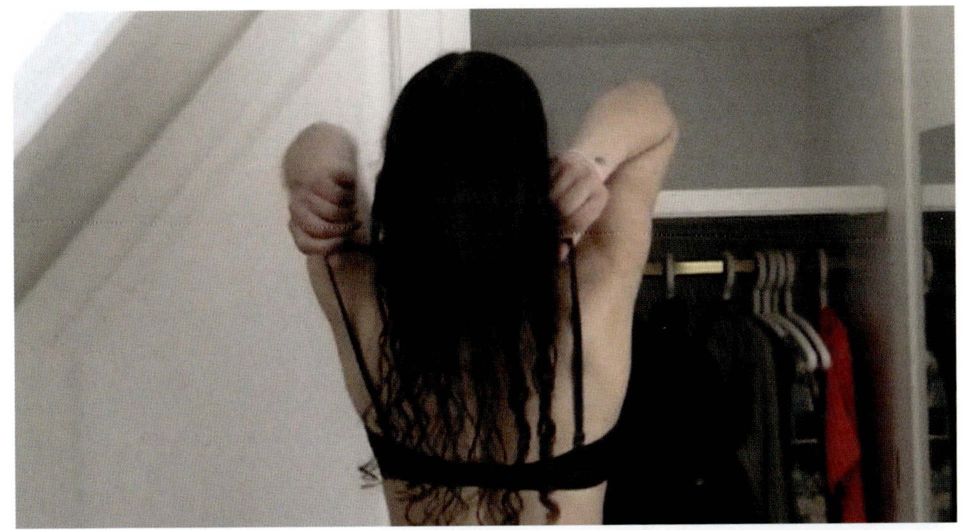

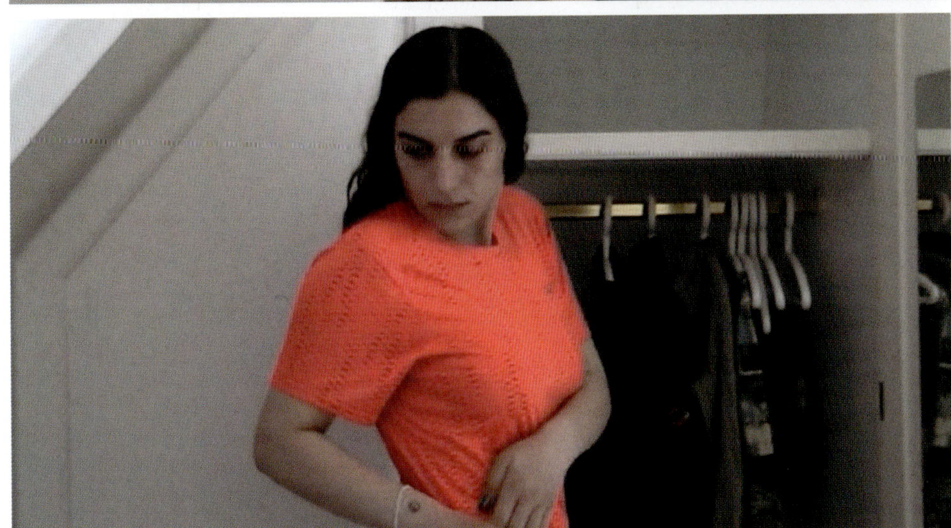

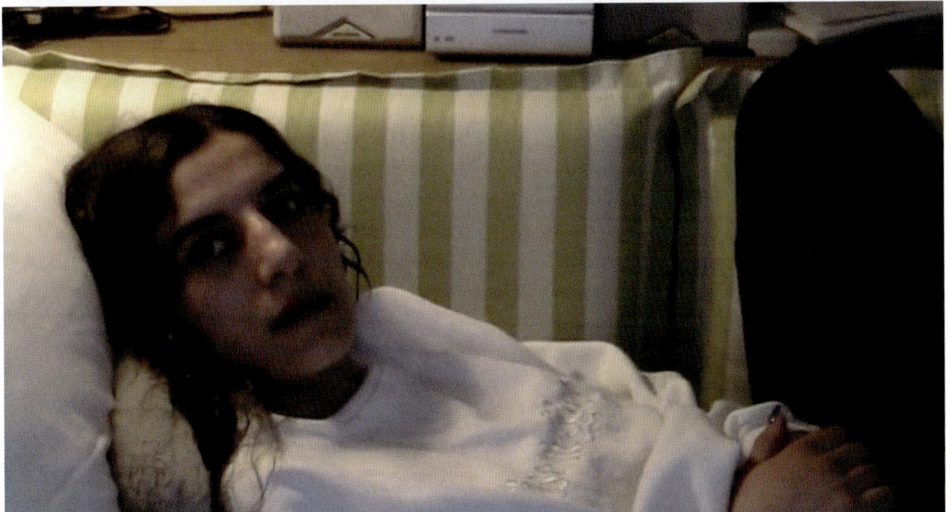

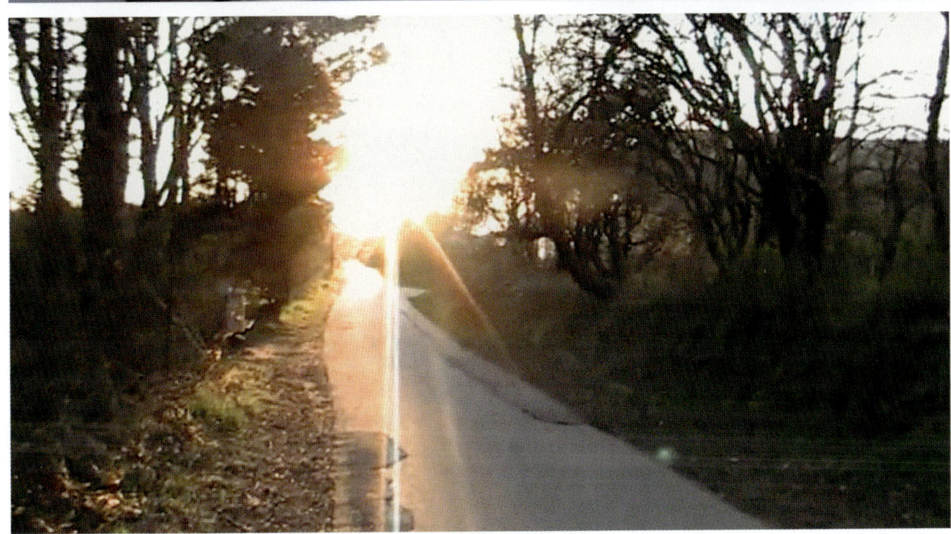

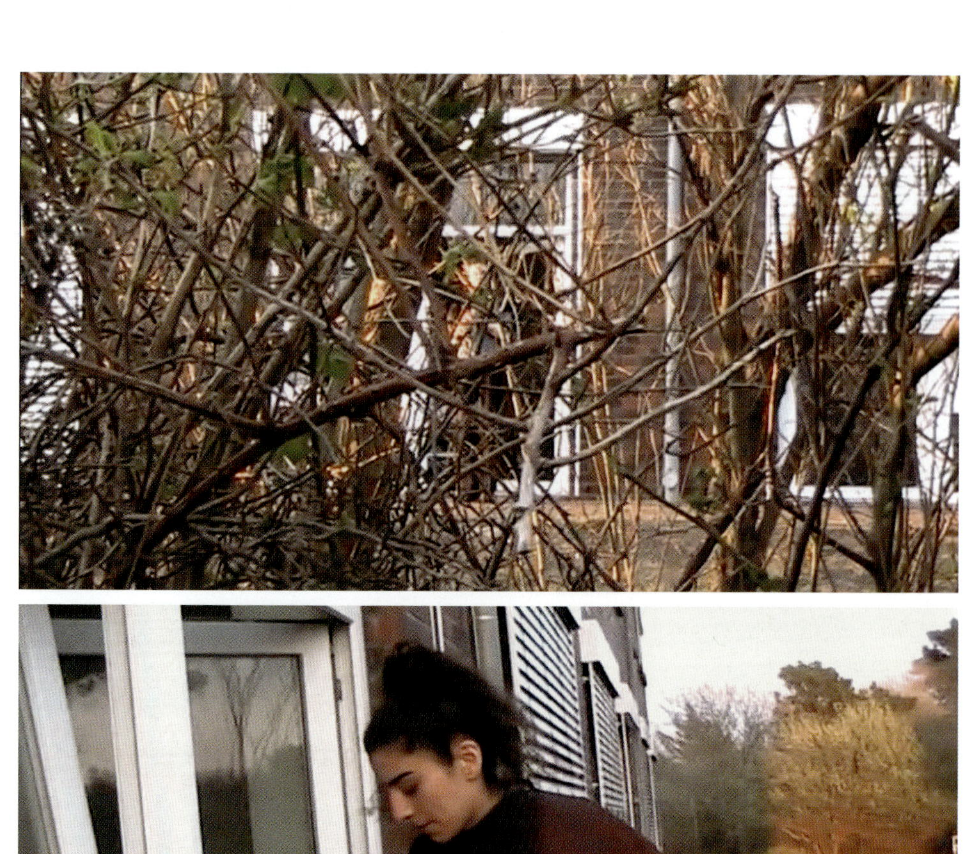
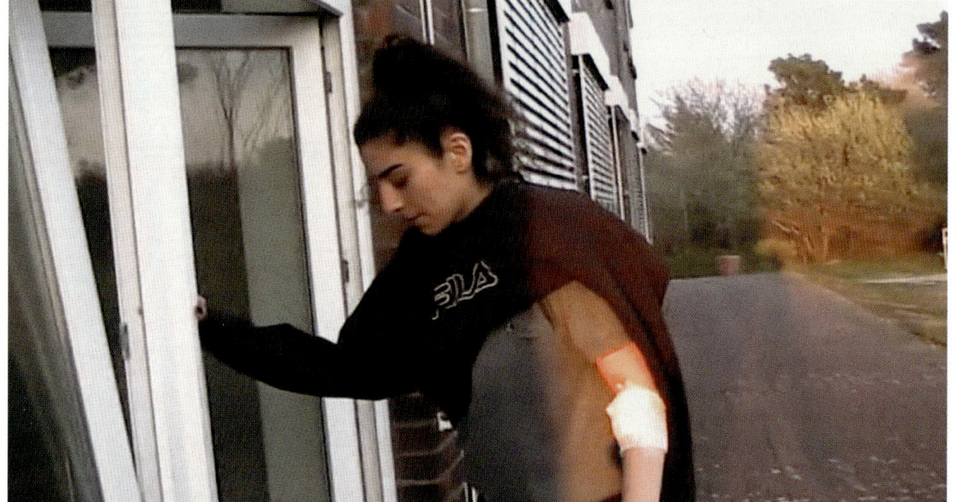
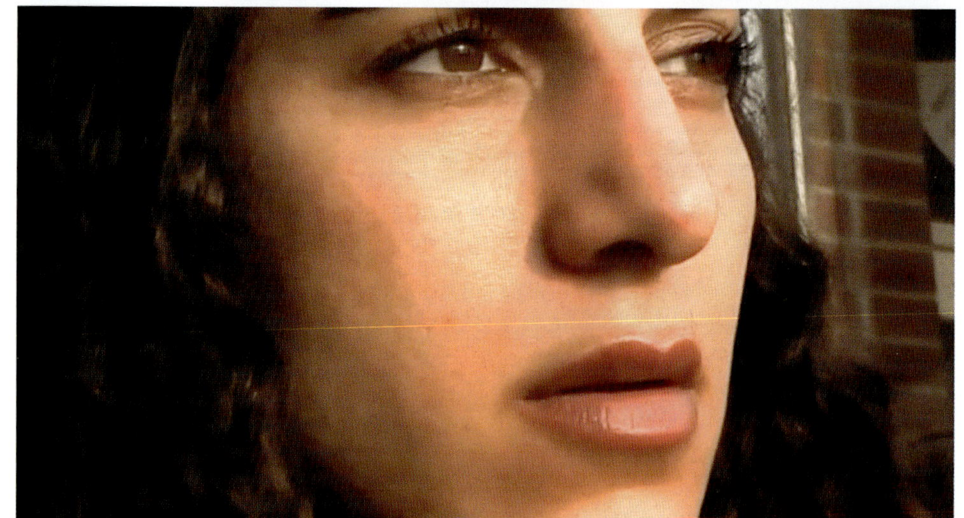
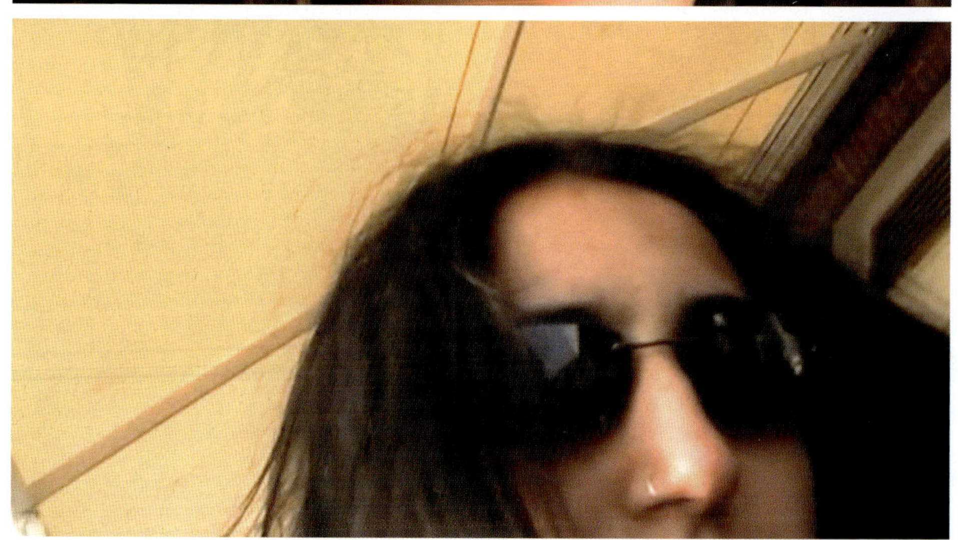

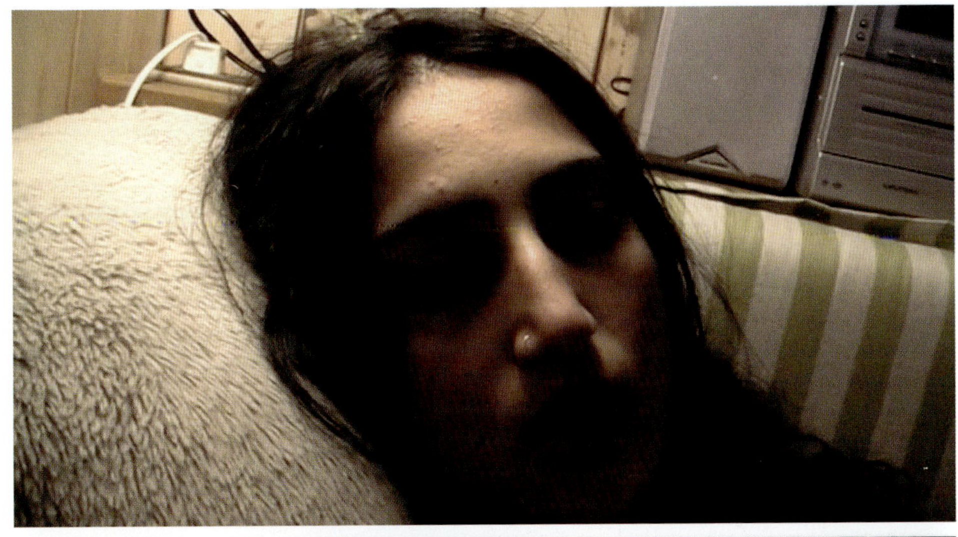

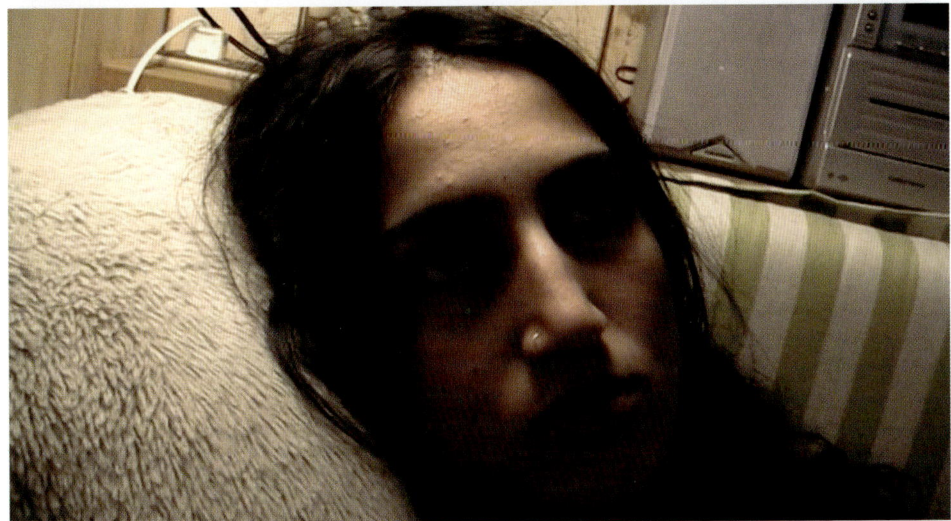

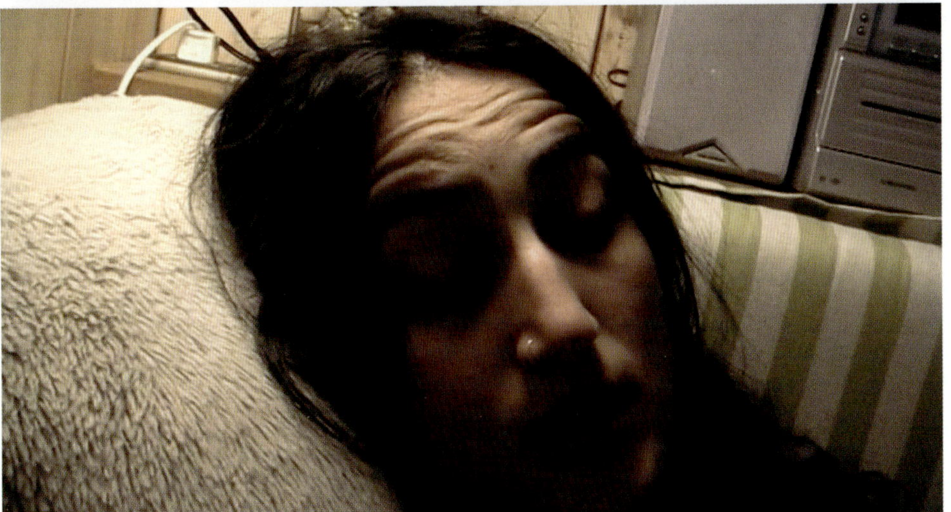

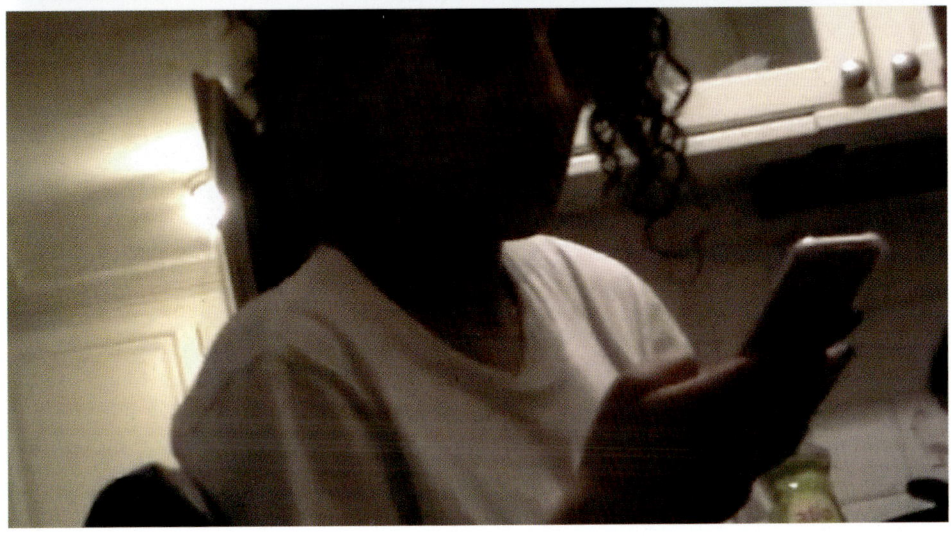

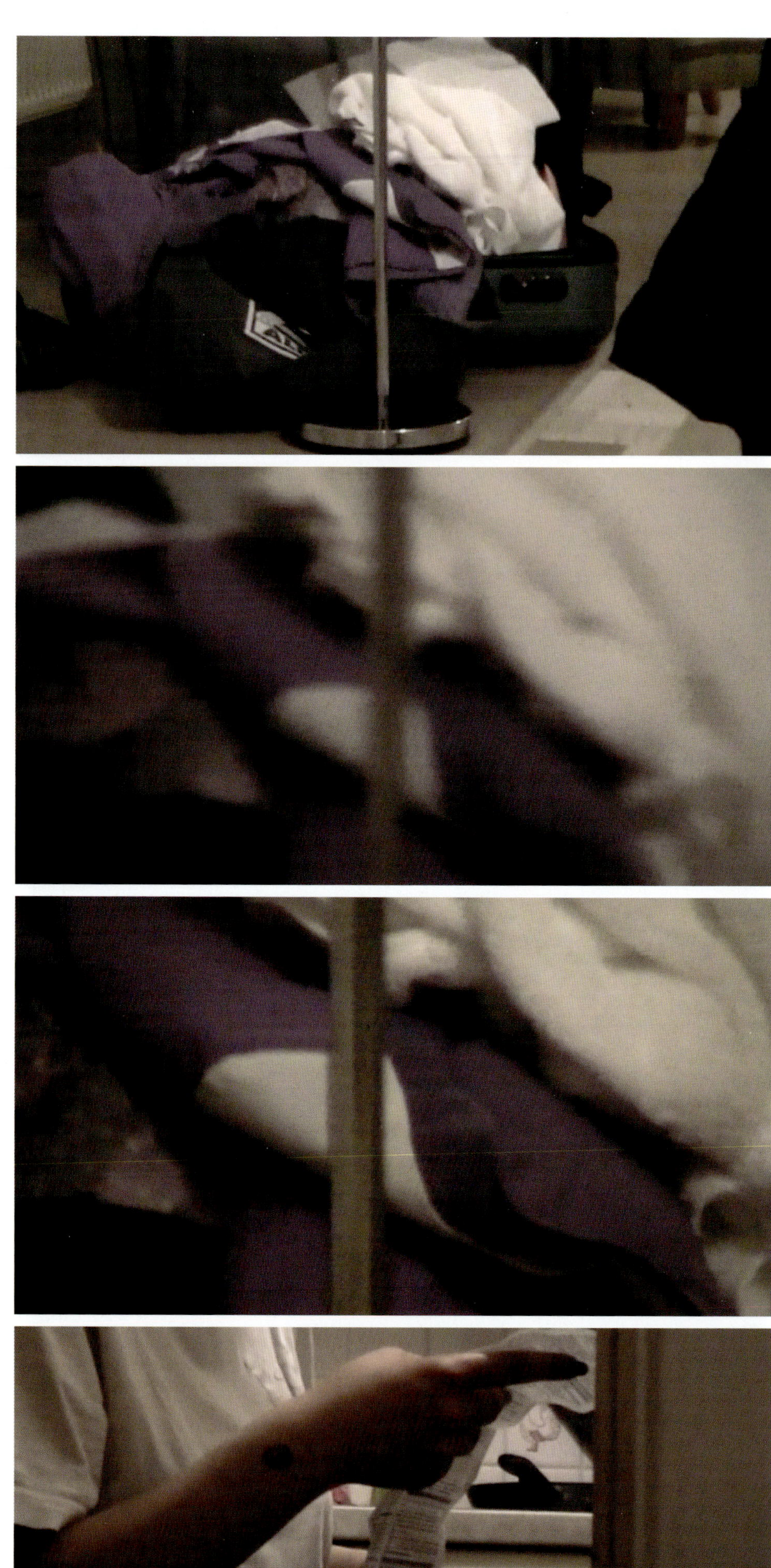

1-7   *Being strong is hard*, 2021
Video, full HD, colour, sound, 4.13 minutes, stills / Video, Full HD,
Farbe, Ton, 4,13 Minuten, Standbilder

26   *Polterabend*, 2022
300 × 200 cm, oil, spray paint and silk-screen printing on canvas /
Öl, Acrylspray und Siebdruck auf Leinwand

27   *Mutig und Hurtig*, 2021
170 × 170 cm, oil, spray paint and silk-screen printing on canvas /
Öl, Acrylspray und Siebdruck auf Leinwand

28   *PlayStation 5*, 2022
300 × 200 cm, oil, spray paint and silk-screen printing on canvas /
Öl, Acrylspray und Siebdruck auf Leinwand

29   *SPCE GRLS*, 2021
190 × 190 cm, oil, spray paint and silk-screen printing on canvas /
Öl, Acrylspray und Siebdruck auf Leinwand

30   *Spice Curls*, 2021
190 × 190 cm, oil, spray paint and silk-screen printing on canvas /
Öl, Acrylspray und Siebdruck auf Leinwand

31   *JBL Xtreme 2 Gun Metal*, 2021
170 × 170 cm, oil, spray paint and silk-screen printing on canvas /
Öl, Acrylspray und Siebdruck auf Leinwand

43-47   *Nacht. Schlaf. Die Sterne.*, 2021
Video installation, full HD, colour, sound, 17.06 minutes, propellers,
stills and installation views / Videoinstallation, Full HD, Farbe, Ton,
17,06 Minuten, Propeller, Standbilder und Installationsansichten,
Kunsthaus Hamburg

48-53   *Bambusel*, 2022
Video, colour, sound, 12.16 minutes, installation views / Video, Farbe,
Ton, 12,16 Minuten, Installationsansichten, Kunsthaus Hamburg

67   *Basement Blues*, 2021
170 × 170 cm, oil, spray paint and silk-screen printing on canvas, detail /
Öl, Acrylspray und Siebdruck auf Leinwand, Detail

68   *Meine Leben*, 2022
280 × 200 cm, oil, spray paint and silk-screen printing on canvas, detail /
Öl, Acrylspray und Siebdruck auf Leinwand, Detail

69   *Alphi-11*, 2022
280 × 200 cm, oil, spray paint and silk-screen printing on canvas, detail /
Öl, Acrylspray und Siebdruck auf Leinwand, Detail

70   *Pink*, 2022
300 × 200 cm, oil, spray paint and silk-screen printing on canvas, detail /
Öl, Acrylspray und Siebdruck auf Leinwand, Detail

71   *Number-1*, 2022
280 × 200 cm, oil, spray paint and silk-screen printing on canvas, detail /
Öl, Acrylspray und Siebdruck auf Leinwand, Detail

72   *PlayStation 5*, 2022
300 × 200 cm, oil, spray paint and silk-screen printing on canvas, detail /
Öl, Acrylspray und Siebdruck auf Leinwand, Detail

74-78   *Bambusel*, 2022
Video, colour, sound, 12.16 minutes, stills / Video, Farbe, Ton,
12,16 Minuten, Standbilder

Courtesy: the artist / die Künstlerin

Photography: Images of paintings and installation views by Hayo Heye,
p. 44 by Claudia Höhne, further material provided by the artist /
Fotografie: Abbildungen von Malereien und Installationsansichten
von Hayo Heye, S. 44 von Claudia Höhne, weiteres Material von
der Künstlerin zur Verfügung gestellt

Nacht. Schlaf. Die Sterne., 2021, supported by: Fonds Darstellende
Künste, the German Federal Government Commissioner for
Culture and the Media (BKM), NEUSTART KULTUR / gefördert von:
Fonds Darstellende Künste aus Mitteln der Beauftragten der
Bundesregierung für Kultur und Medien (BKM) im Rahmen von
NEUSTART KULTUR

Exhibition / Ausstellung

**LEYLA YENIRCE
SO MUCH ENERGY**
15.10.–4.12.2022

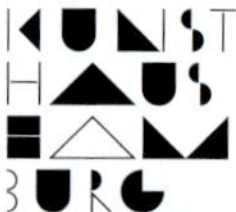

Kunsthaus Hamburg
Klosterwall 15
20095 Hamburg
info@kunsthaushamburg.de
www.kunsthaushamburg.de

Managing and Artistic Director /
Geschäftsführung und künstlerische Leitung
Katja Schroeder

Curator / Kuratorin
Anna Nowak

Public Relations / Presse- und
Öffentlichkeitsarbeit
Elena Weickmann

Accounting / Buchhaltung
Reni Pathak

Internship / Praktikum
Corinna Sarić, Fenia Scholl

Associates / Gesellschafter
Griffelkunst-Vereinigung e.V.,
Neue Kunst in Hamburg e.V.,
BBK – Berufsverband Bildender
KünstlerInnen Hamburg e.V.,
Frank Otto

Supported by / Mit Unterstützung von

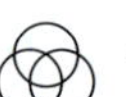
Alfried Krupp von Bohlen
und Halbach-Stiftung

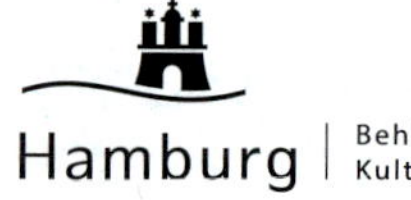
hamburgische
kulturstiftung

Hamburg | Behörde für
Kultur und Medien

Imprint / Impressum

LEYLA YENIRCE
SO MUCH ENERGY

Kunsthaus Hamburg

Published and distributed by /
Herausgegeben und vertrieben von
Mousse Publishing
Contrappunto s.r.l.
via Pier Candido Decembrio 28,
20137, Milan–Italy

Available through / Erhältlich über
    Mousse Publishing, Milan
    moussemagazine.it
DAP | Distributed
Art Publishers, New York
artbook.com
    Les presses du réel, Dijon
    lespressesdureel.com
    Antenne Books, London
    antennebooks.com
    Idea Books, Amsterdam
    ideabooks.nl

Editor / Herausgeber
Kunsthaus Hamburg

Texts / Texte
Enis Maci, Mazlum Nergiz,
Anna Nowak

Concept / Konzept
Mousse Publishing
Anna Nowak, Leyla Yenirce

Design / Gestaltung
Massimiliano Pace (Mousse)

Publishing editor / Leiterin der
Publikationsabteilung
Ilaria Bombelli (Mousse)

Translation / Übersetzung
Belinda Grace Gardner,
Barbara Lang

Editing / Lektorat
Barbara Lang, Nina Mentrup,
Anna Nowak

Print / Druck
Ancora Arti Grafiche, Milano

ISBN 978-88-6749-552-8
€ 25 / $ 29.95

The publisher would like to thank all those who have kindly given their permission for the reproduction of material for this book. Every effort has been made to obtain permission to reproduce the images and texts in this catalogue. However, as is standard editorial policy, the publisher is at the disposal of copyright holders and undertakes to correct any omissions or errors in future editions.

Der Verlag bedankt sich bei all jenen, die freundlicherweise der Reproduktion von Material in dieser Publikation zugestimmt haben. Es wurden alle Bemühungen unternommen, um die Genehmigung zur Wiedergabe der Bilder und Texte in diesem Katalog zu erhalten. Der Verlag steht wie immer den Inhabern der Urheberrechte zur Disposition und verpflichtet sich, etwaige Auslassungen oder Fehler in künftigen Ausgaben zu korrigieren.

Thanks to / Danke an
Marvin Moises Almaraz Dosal, Ilaria Bombelli, Anders Fallesen, Alessio Gentile, Hayo Heye, Marlene Lockemann, Ingmar Mruk, Massimiliano Pace, Dr. Karin Schick, Hannes Schmidt, Katja Schroeder, Heinz Völlen, Esmer Yenirce.

We are grateful to the Alfried Krupp von Bohlen and Halbach Foundation for supporting Leyla Yenirce with their programme "Catalogues for Young Artists" and enabling her to release her catalogue and exhibition project.

Vielen Dank an die Alfried Krupp von Bohlen und Halbach-Stiftung für die Ermöglichung der Ausstellung und des Kataloges im Rahmen des Förderpreises „Kataloge für junge Künstler*innen".

The artist would like to thank everyone who was involved in the artistic productions depicted in this catalogue. First of all Enis Maci and Mazlum Nergiz whom the artist met a decade ago as collaborators and friends for a lifetime, Theresa George who always succeeds in leading a project into the right direction with a unique brain and eye, with pleasure, austerity and joy, Kuno Seltmann for his unconditional help, love and editing skills, Kris Jakob for being a versatile mastermind when it comes to sound, Janosa Mike for being an astonishing, unpredictable actress, Sin Huh for his camera work and elaborate technical expertise, Prateek Viyan and Ulf Freyhoff for engineering the ever-spinning propellers, Karsten Witte for engineering the steal work, Helix Propeller GmbH for being such generous supporters in sponsoring the handcrafted propellers, Anna Nowak for her invitation and help, and again Mazlum Nergiz who inspired to the title of the work *Nacht. Schlaf. Die Sterne.* that was taken from his theater play *1000 Eyes*.

Die Künstlerin möchte allen danken, die an den Produktionen, die in diesem Katalog abgebildet sind, beteiligt waren. Allen voran Enis Maci und Mazlum Nergiz, die sie vor einer Dekade als Kollaborateure auf Lebenszeit kennengelernt hat; Theresa George, der es immer wieder gelingt, ein Projekt einzigartig und visionär, mit Lust und Strenge in die richtige Richtung zu lenken; Kuno Seltmann für seine bedingungslose Hilfe und Schnittkompetenz; Kris Jakob als vielseitiges Mastermind des Klangs; Janosa Mike als erstaunliche, unberechenbare Schauspielerin, Sin Huh für seine Kameraarbeit und sein ausgeklügeltes technisches Fachwissen; Prateek Viyan und Ulf Freyhoff für die Konstruktion der sich permanent drehenden Propeller; Karsten Witte für die Gestaltung der Stahlarbeiten; Helix-Carbon GmbH für die großzügige Unterstützung beim Sponsoring der handgefertigten Propeller, Anna Nowak für ihre Einladung und Hilfe und erneut Mazlum Nergiz, der zum Titel des Werkes *Nacht. Schlaf. Die Sterne.*, der aus seinem Theaterstück *1000 Eyes* entnommen ist, inspiriert hat.